ENDORSEMENTS

Three months after I arrived from Guatemala to study in La Esmeralda, with a scholarship from the democratic government, I was asked to work as an assistant on Diego Rivera's mural *Dream of a Sunday Afternoon in Alameda Central Park*. Diego was starting the mural in the Hotel del Prado where the famous phrase "God does not exist" scandalized Mexico.

A year after, I was able to assist the genius in "his labyrinth" and to listen to the corpulent maestro dressed in denim overalls speak to Alfredo Cardona Peña. We called the writer *jucjhitico*, for having been married to a beautiful woman from *Juchitan*, Oaxaca, and *tico* for being from Costa Rica, one of the most beautiful places in Central America.

The union of these talented men allowed Alfredo Cardona Peña to capture in this book—with sarcasm, knowledge, wisdom, and ingenuity—anecdotes and experiences of Diego's artistic, intellectual, and political life in Mexico and the world. I witnessed the birth of this book take place in front of a picture window in the maestro's beautiful studio in San Angel, through which a green-yellow foliage peeked, Diego Rivera's favorite color, and mixed with the Congo-green of the floor In this ambiance, I heard the writer ask targeted questions. I was still very young, enjoying and learning by listening, while I discretely muffled a smile.

—Rina Lazo, painter and last living student of Diego Rivera

When Rina painted the mural *The Four Elements*, the critics applauded her . . . even the painters. Needless to say, Diego saw her as the apple of his eye

—María Luisa, La China Mendoza

"If art is not made, there is a danger of death," Diego Rivera tells us in this splendid book, which is itself a powerful argument for life, and for the kinds of vital, authentic art without which fully human lives are impossible. These pages are practically bursting with Rivera's colossal genius, and his words, reaching us only now in English after almost 70 years, are as necessary today as they were in 1950. Read this book; your heart, your soul, and your mind will all thank you for it.

—Ben Fountain, author of *Billy Lynn's Long Halftime Walk*, winner of the National Book Critics' Circle Award and finalist for the National Book Award

This book is a marvelous stroll with Mexican artist Diego Rivera, a gift offered by Alfredo Cardona Peña with empathy, intelligence, and an infinite curiosity for Mexico—its indigenous and popular culture, art as propaganda, and painting as boundless energy. Rivera is rendered in full flesh: combative, keen, urgent and vital.

—Gabriel Trujillo Muñoz, author of *Mezquite Road*

The appearance in English of these wide-ranging and brilliant interviews of Mexico's greatest painter, Diego Rivera, by Alfredo Cordona Peña is a triumph for all who wish to understand the Mexican master. In this case, the writer was respected so much by the artist that the results are a kind of dance between two equals. The elegant translation by the writer's brother, Alvaro Cardona-Hine, is an act of homage that makes these interviews, known to every scholar of Rivera's work in Spanish, accessible to a wider audience in English. The resulting text is very much like Paul Gauguin's wide-ranging last book, *Avant et Après*, and a book less about art than about history, art history, aesthetics, politics, literature, the art market, and memory. It is filled with surprising stories, fiercely held opinions, and a kind of intellectual swagger perfectly captured in its subtitle "The Monster in his Labyrinth"

—Richard R. Brettell, PhD, Founding Director,
the Edith O'Donnell Institute of Art History
and the Margaret McDermott Distinguished
Chair, the University of Texas at Dallas

CONVERSATIONS with DIEGO RIVERA

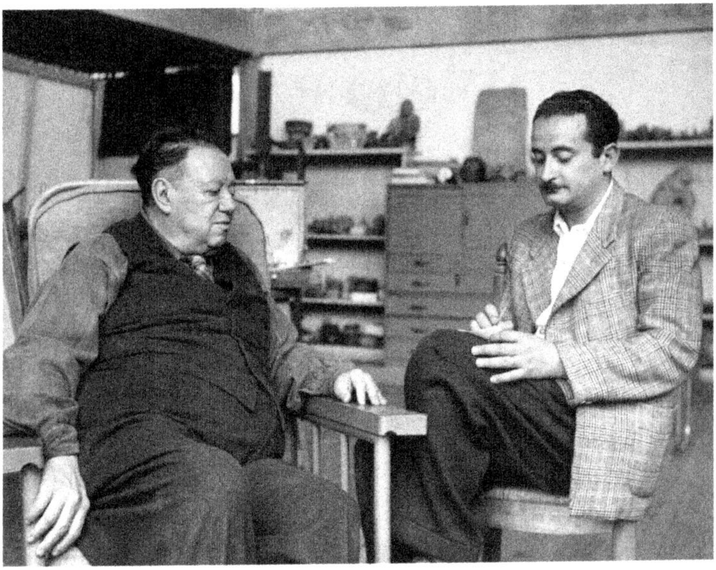

CONVERSATIONS with DIEGO RIVERA

THE MONSTER IN HIS LABYRINTH

by Alfredo Cardona Peña

A translation by Alvaro Cardona-Hine
of *El Monstruo en su Laberinto*

New Village Press • New York

Published in the United States by
New Village Press
bookorders@newvillagepress.net
www.newvillagepress.net
New Village Press is a public-benefit, not-for-profit publisher.
Distributed by New York University Press
newvillagepress.nyupress.org

Paperback ISBN-13: 978-1-61332-032-7
Publication Date: July 9, 2018
First English Edition

Library of Congress Cataloging-in-Publication Data

Names: Cardona Peäna, Alfredo, interviewer. | Rivera, Diego, 1886-1957, interviewee. | Cardona-Hine, Alvaro, translator. | Translation of: Cardona Peäna, Alfredo. Monstruo en su laberinto.
Title: Conversations with Diego Rivera : the monster in his labyrinth / by Alfredo Cardona Peäna ; a translation by Alvaro Cardona-Hine of El monstruo en su laberinto.
Other titles: Monstruo en su laberinto. English
Description: First English edition. | New York : New Village Press, 2018.
Identifiers: LCCN 2018013868| ISBN 9781613320327 (pbk.) | ISBN 9781613320297 (hardcover)
Subjects: LCSH: Rivera, Diego, 1886-1957—Interviews. | Painters—Mexico—Interviews.
Classification: LCC ND259.R5 A35 2018 | DDC 759.972—dc 3
LC record available at https://lccn.loc.gov/2018013868

Front cover photo: Diego Rivera in his studio, July 30, 1950, Diego Rivera (III), c.1949 (gelatin silver print), Alvarez Bravo, Lola (1907–93) / Detroit Institute of Arts, USA / Founders Society Purchase, Diego Rivera Exhibition Fund / Bridgeman Images
Frontispiece: Diego Rivera and Alfredo Cardona Peña, July 30, 1950, by Lola Alvarez Bravo, courtesy Cora Cardona.
Page 159: Diego Rivera, *Young Boy with a Bucket*, 1934, by permission of Harvard Art Museums/Fogg Museum. Dark gray watercolor on cream rice paper; 39 x 28 cm (15⅜ x 11 in.) Harvard Art Museums/Fogg Museum, Gift of Louis W. Black, 1955 © Diego Rivera / Artist Rights Society (ARS), New York. Photo: Imaging Department © President and Fellows of Harvard College
Cover design: Lynne Elizabeth
Interior design and composition: Leigh McLellan

CONTENTS

TRANSLATOR'S PREFACE

A FEW WORDS about my half-brother Alfredo's background and life as a Latin American poet and journalist might be of interest to the English-speaking readers of this book.

Alfredo, born on August 11, 1917, died before the turn of the century.

We are a literary Costa Rican family on my paternal side, with five of us, in three generations, published writers.

Alfredo's mother was from El Salvador. My father married her in spite of knowing she was ill with tuberculosis. She died in Costa Rica when Alfredo was about three years old and he was raised by our paternal aunts, Graciela and Odilie, until he went to Salvador to stay with his maternal family and finish his schooling. After a short visit to Costa Rica, he went to Mexico where he became a journalist, married Alba Chacón, a beautiful and bright Zapotec Indian woman with whom he had two children, Alfredo, his son (today a painter), and Cora (a successful actress and theatre director in Dallas).

Early in life Alfredo manifested great poetic talent. In Mexico he found his true home, developed his talents, and went on to write more than twenty books of poetry and prose. An amiable and well-connected man, he knew Spanish poets in exile such as José Moreno Villa and Leon Felipe. Pablo Neruda called his poetry "*desbordante y solar*" (boundless and solar).

The dedication on the 111th copy of the Rivera book he gave me reads, "To my brother Alvaro, who will translate this book into the English language. Mexico D. F. August 27 / 71."

It is with deep regret that it is only now, in 2015, at the age of 88, that I have attempted to translate my beloved brother's work. I dedicate my labors to his memory.

INTRODUCTION

IN SEPTEMBER OF 1948, Diego Rivera escaped being lynched by a mob of hotheads stoning his house in *Coyoacán*. In his mural at the Prado Hotel, in Mexico City, the artist had reproduced a phrase by the liberal writer Ignacio Ramírez (1818-1879) sufficiently strong to ignite the ire of malcontents.

The phrase that provoked the riot read, in bold letters: **God doesn't exist**. The hotel management, frightened, ordered the mural to be covered up. The title of the mural was, *Dream of a Sunday Afternoon in the Alameda Central Park*. The then archbishop of Mexico, Doctor Luis María Martinez, for his part, refused to bless the new hotel and the clergy attacked Rivera from the pulpit. The word spread that the building was damned and destined to burn. Rivera was delighted.

Many years before, when the artist was in Toledo, Spain (1907), the legend spread among folk that "he fed on the bones of children." That may have been what led to the famous attempt on his life.

He shook up the newspapers twenty years ago spreading the version that he was a cannibal. I heard him say, to a group of students in the state of Puebla, "human meat has a slightly sweet taste, superior to that of any edible animal." The students were horrified. Diego laughed to himself.

When his third wife, Frida Kahlo, that extraordinary painter, died, her wake was held in the Palace of Bellas Artes, as a proper homage to her work. Diego arrived and ordered the unfurling of a flag with the hammer and sickle, and the Communists, headed by him, sang "The Internationale." Such was the scandal that it led to the downfall of the director of the National Institute of Bellas Artes, the writer Andrés Iduarte. Rivera rubbed his hands in glee.

One time I asked him, "how would you decorate the Mexico City Cathedral?" The reply was devastating: "The day that Mexico's cathedral is turned into a useful building, no longer the provider of opium to the people, and it is turned into a discussion center, a popular museum, a garrison, a library or grain cellar, I would love nothing more than to decorate it. If Mexican Catholics had any sense, they would ask their bankers of the Committee on Decorum to hire José Clemente Orozco or myself to work on a series of works that would turn the cathedral into a visual center of such importance that those hotels whose investors are the same bankers from the Committee, would do the most fantastic business of their lives."

Because of such views, Diego Rivera was continuously insulted in the press, in public when he ventured to espouse one of his radical theories, and privately when traditional notions were offended by his declarations, manifestos or communications.

But when the government organized the exposition of his complete works, celebrating his fifty years of artistic labor, he was declared "one of the greatest painters in the history of Mexico and one of the few authentic world-wide greats of the present time." The select minorities who witnessed the exhibition backed up that declaration as being no exaggeration.

When the papers announced the news of his death, the 25th of September 1957, the people, now *en masse*, put in an appearance before his remains. Multitudes invaded Bellas Artes where a funeral chapel was set up. Men of all ideologies and social position made the long trek from the center of town to the Dolores Cemetery, where he was buried in the Rotunda of Illustrious Men.

For three days, Diego Rivera owned the eight columns that newspapers reserve for sensational news. Columnists, editorialists and graphic artists paid him homage, praising his work. The same press that had hounded him now praised him unanimously. And Diego Rivera, the "dangerous Communist," went to his grave covered by the national flag in the midst of the consternation of the whole country.

Rivera initiated the mural movement in our time, giving the work of art a public destiny since it is realized, not on the canvas of private collectors, but on the walls of buildings that are the property of the nation.

In 1922, he finished his first mural at the National Preparatory School in Mexico City with a philosophic theme he entitled *The Creation*. From that year to the year of his death, the measurement of the surfaces he painted comes to 30,000 square meters, an amount not realized by any other artist in the world.

The mural work represents the culmination of his experiences in the field of art, the maturity of his life, and the synthesis of the various schools of painting that he knew and mastered.

In his early youth, when he was a student at the San Carlos Academy, he quickly broke with the academic tradition and looked for the free expression of his ideas. He took up Spanish realism, was immensely moved by Cezanne, and managed to conquer, successively, the techniques of all modern tendencies: Impressionism, Cubism, Futurism, Surrealism, all of which he enriched with new contributions during his travels in Europe, especially in Paris, where he exhibited at the *Salon des Independents* and the famous *Salon d'Autumne.*

He had a surprising capacity for work; in 70 years of professional life he was able to finish several thousand pictures: watercolors, oils, ink drawings, pastels, pencil items, frescoes, etc., involving, all together, hundreds of millions of dollars in value.

When I asked him how many hours a day he spent at work he replied, "The time varies a lot, but almost always I go for the longest possible amount, generally from 10 to 14 hours a day."

I was able to verify this affirmation seeing how in 1950 he started work on his fourth mural at the National Palace, representing a scene with the agricultural god *Yacatecuhtli.* He began on a Thursday at seven a.m. and he didn't rest until nine o'clock the next morning, with the exception of a seven-hour break, after which he worked the night through until close to dawn Saturday.

Everything about Diego Rivera was monstrous: the way he worked, the way he'd insult, love and suffer. But his monstrousness originated deep down in the flame of his heart, the bottomless tenderness of genetic clay. He is comparable to Luther. The two come from downtrodden social classes, proud to be "sons of peasants." Their fathers were both miners connected to the middle classes. Rivera and Luther are "energies erupting from the earth, like craters suddenly exploding," according to the expression of Alfred Weber when referring to the father of the German Reformation.

Diego Rivera springs like a geyser out of the Mexican soil and starts to paint the way an Aztec god would do it in the days of human sacrifice, bloodied and filled with amazing vitality. D. H. Lawrence compared Rivera with the terrible *Tezcatlipoca*, solar and ecumenical deity of ancient Mexico.

In truth, we can identify this painter with each of the deities that form the Aztec pantheon: with *Tlaloc,* god of water; with *Quetzalcoatl,* beneficent god of light; with the profound *Coatlicue,* goddess of earth and death, portrayed with eagle claws and a skirt of snakes.

The writer Fernando Benítez tells how, after being up on a scaffold for three days working on the hands of a colossal figure, Diego Rivera fell to the ground and was taken home more dead than alive. Explaining this accident, his assistants said he had been pushed by the hands of the god he had just finished painting. Once, referring to pre-Hispanic idols he said, "They are my nourishment."

One day, talking with him about his family, I learned that it had included "bandits, priests, military men and revolutionaries." Diego Rivera was born on the 8th of December 1886, from that severe mix, at eight o'clock at night, in the mining town of Guanajuato, Pocitos Street number 8.

It's necessary to look at the initial branches of his genealogy. His grandparents come from many places: Italy, Russia, Portugal, Holland, from Veracruz and San Miguel de Allende.

His paternal grandparents were Anastasio de la Rivera Sforza, an Italian Jew born in Russia from an unknown mother, and Inés d'Acosta, a Portuguese Jew who emigrated to Holland. His maternal grandparents were Juan Barrientos, originally from Alvarado, Veracruz, and Nemesia Rodríguez Valpuesta, from San Miguel de Allende, Guanajuato, Mexico. His parents were Diego Rivera, dead from cancer at age 75, and María Barrientos y Rodríguez Valpuesta, dead at 63, also from cancer.

Diego Rivera contains in his blood a cocktail of maps whose olive is Mexico. It should be imbibed slowly to avoid sudden intoxication.

As one of his critics has said, "He was born under the sign of events with contradictory symbolism: just as, in Mexico, General Porfirio Díaz reelects himself to a second term in office, in New York, the Statue of Liberty is inaugurated at the mouth of the Hudson."

• • •

The artist was 63 years old when I began interviewing him. He was then a corpulent man, with a big belly, wearing huge pigskin shoes, overalls, coats of ordinary material and checkered wool shirts. He was careless in his attire but moved with delicacy and elegance, with a smile on his face that could pass for mockery, irony or sadness. He weighed more than 90 kilos, and he carried that weight high up scaffolds, working whole days without coming down, struggling like a demon.

His breakfast consisted of bananas, pears, apples and a cup of green tea while in the evening he'd eat the standard Mexican meal: noodle soup, meat stew and dessert. He opted for an oriental way of eating, and in his last years he went from using knives and forks to chopsticks. I always thought that in some recess of his being there was a hidden bonze or a lama who "hung up his Himalayas" and came to America, perhaps in a Viking ship.

Ramón Gómez de la Serna, in a much admired article about the master, said that when he showed up in Madrid, "he had the look of an authentic living Buddha, with the sumptuous fatness of the Buddha," and that his eyes evoked "the awful look of one of his forebears."

That is true. The first thing that impressed one about his face were those bulging eyes, ready to pop out of their orbits. From so much absorbing light and the colors of the world, those windows of the soul had been damaged a bit so when the morning would stream in, they'd redden and weep. These pathetic eyes seemed to swing free of their location and follow the attentive observer. In his self-portraits, Rivera emphasized their condition, which is why those faces he came up with are so tremendously intense.

His right eye was operated on in 1934 because of an atrophied ulcer caused by a streptococcus infection. The lachrymal gland in the upper section of the orbit was removed so that thereafter it was unable to retain any fluid; it would tear from time to time. After many hours working with the strong colors he preferred, that sick eye needed rest but the painter wouldn't give in. It is no exaggeration to say that when Rivera painted he wept.

In his eyes the passion for art was stigmatized. It was only after he died that his eyes settled back to a normal position, shrouded now by the darkness they may have always yearned for.

Rivera detested cigarette smoke. He papered his studio with huge posters stating the familiar "No Smoking, Please." He worked in the midst of great shafts of light, and when it was artificial it was so strong as to be blinding when one first entered the room.

We shall always remember those "bug eyes, held back by bloated, salient lids like those of a batrachian," as Frida Kahlo used to say.

• • •

In 1949, the Mexican president opened the Diego Rivera exposition at the Museum of Plastic Arts at the Palace of Bellas Artes to commemorate fifty years of Rivera's work. Hundreds of works were shown on that occasion, starting with his first drawing, (*The Railroad*, 1889) made at age three, and ending with photographs of his last murals from the National Palace.

Diego Rivera was revealed to his people, unfamiliar as yet with him, as a true master of all historical styles of art. Ignorant men, who are legion, used to call him "a nobody." One of them, a boorish gentleman, decided one Sunday to visit the much talked about exposition and was struck dumb. He understood nothing, of course, but underwent a shift of consciousness. He had to take off his hat before an artist so often maligned.

• • •

When it comes to technical matters, we shall refer only to his experiments and research into wax painting, better known as encaustic painting, whose most notable exponent was Delacroix (Lateral chapels of the Church of Saint Sulpice in Paris).

Rivera himself, following the exposition, discussed his own research into encaustic and al fresco techniques with the Mexican painter Juan O'Gorman. Here is the crux of the matter, revealing of the scientific and humanistic fervor of the artist: "I began to get interested," he told his friend, "with wax and resin color around 1905, above all with the idea of substituting it for oil color, as Raphael did. In those days that was the novelty and excitement among painters working with the neo-impressionist tendencies, like the great Seurat and the Swiss-Italian Segantini. Nobody had found the procedure to cauterize and arrive at the proper encaustic means. So I resolved to go to the sources, which were Greek, Coptic, Egyptian and Roman, but these kept the secret of such painting a mystery. And so it was. There was nothing else to do but take recourse in Pliny's writings on natural history. There is one chapter where he talks of painting methods. Montavert, Delacroix and others had consulted Pliny without success so I, with the audacity of one who knows nothing and lacks respect for classic authors, thought it might be a question of how to interpret the Latin text, and went to look for it at the National Library in Paris. Montavert said that Pliny mentioned encaustic as 'an oil of pine and stone.' Of course, nobody understood what that was all about. When I came upon that specific passage in Pliny I could hardly believe what I was reading. The key word was petroleum. Petroleum in Pliny's time could only be obtained through exudation or in natural springs. What Pliny meant was really 'hide,' which Montavert had translated as 'pine.'

"Then I remembered that in the Caucasus and Asia Minor, way before Pliny, petroleum was obtained by placing the hide of lambs on fields exuding petroleum. But there was another issue pending, the most important: how to cauterize it. About this Pliny said 'For fine work, painters use the torches of gold and silversmiths.' That reminded me of the silversmiths of my childhood in Mexico, how they used a lamp loaded with petroleum, blowing into its flame with a metal blowgun and sending it to a base of clay where the metal they wanted to melt lay. In other words, the mysterious torch that confused Leonardo da Vinci was nothing other than a common lead blowgun. I tried this approach over ground colors in an emulsion of copal oil and wax dissolved in an essence of petroleum and was able to obtain the result used by the old masters, reincorporating the encaustic procedure into modern art."

What about the aesthetics of his painting? Let us hear what the philosopher Samuel Ramos has to say:

"Diego Rivera's aesthetic begins with the assumption that art must be the expression of an ideological content determined by the social conditions of the moment in which the artist lives. The notion of art for art's sake is, for Rivera, a mask hiding the pursuit of interests other than artistic. The political basis he has given his work blinds his opponents, keeping them from seeing and judging its plastic values. As a human being, Diego Rivera has involved himself in the social struggles of our time; he has actively joined leftist causes. His painting involves a political thesis. His entire mural achievement is the visual objectification of a socialist idea based on Mexican history. It is not proper to discuss his political notions when considering Diego Rivera's painting. What can be discussed is whether the procedure of using painting as the instrument of an ideological expression can be legitimized from an aesthetic point of view.

"If someone looks into Rivera's work for the ideal of beauty as formulated at a certain period of European art, which has been turned into a kind of universal model, that person is wasting his time. It seems to me that the true universal conscience of art ought to be one that denies the right to grant privileges to a specific form of beauty at the expense of others, recognizing the existence of multiple forms through which different epochs, different peoples and diverse individuals, have found that same spiritual pleasure that confers unity to the perception of what we call beauty. What distinguishes Rivera's painting from its European counterpart is precisely an original manner of seeing and grouping the diverse plastic elements provided by a reality as peculiar as that of the Mexican people, heretofore unknown in the world of art. Its aesthetic value is realized by the authenticity with which the painter has known how to capture the personal features of his people and his environment, as well as by the fidelity of the artist to his own manner of seeing and thinking."

Relating to the initial influences on Rivera, his spiritual connection to the great masters and the discovery of his own world, let us see what Germaine Wenziner has to say:

"No sooner had he arrived in Europe than he visited the museums, diving into Assyrian and archaic Greek art. He stopped in front of the blues of Fray Angelico, wandering long among the primitives. He leaped into the sobriety of Courbet, yet surrendered more deeply to the charm of the *Moulin de la Galette*, was unsettled by the musical structures that Renoir had created between the palpitating life in his drawings and his vibrant chromatics. Every art manifestation shook him. He suffered the authoritarian presence of David's portraits, returned to the impressionists, the neo-impressionists. Afterwards, discovering Seurat, he thought he'd go crazy. Nevertheless, it was Cézanne who made the deepest impression. What affects one the most in studying the life of Diego Rivera during that period is his extraordinary expenditure of energy and the excitement in this foreign painter ready to discover everything that the pictorial universe could be hiding. His genius was like a demon punishing him without respite."

Crespo de la Serna lists some key moments when Rivera found his creative conscience. Certainly his encounter with the work of Cézanne at the *boutique* of Ambroise Vollard, "an impact that in spite of his flight to other artistic premises and his devotion to El Greco, left an important mark on his spirit and even more on the on-going gestation of his art." His dealings with Cubism "in which he managed to attain a clear presence and which he later transformed into a constructivist system based on previous experiences." His visit to Italy (frescoes from the Renaissance, the work of the primitives, etc.) "from which he derived his resolve to paint murals in the future." Lastly, "his re-discovery of the Mexico intuited in his childhood and adolescence, when he returned to his country for the second time in 1921."

After his cubist period, Rivera left Paris a mature artist.

"Fifteen years away from his homeland," says Wenziner, "had made him a more absolute Mexican than he had ever been. Like Flaubert, who, during a trip, conceived Madame Bovary as a type of woman different from those of other places, in the same way Diego Rivera, during his stay in Paris, meditated and conceived his great Mexican masterpieces."

This re-discovery of Mexico gave the painter a unique originality, thanks to which he reached the stage of a definitive awareness as an artist, painting his land with a chromatic and incomparable force. So, this entire process, all this evolution from his beginnings to the time of his major conceptions, was presented in the exposition of 1949, the supreme triumph of his life in front of his people. He actually filled all the salons of the Palace of Bellas Artes. The amazed public went from one period to the next, confirming silently the total revelation of his genius. Afterwards... afterwards came what we may call an evening with the sun on the horizon. Rivera gave himself up to painting with the fury of the possessed, just painting, painting. He painted at all hours of the day and night, at home, in his studio, in the street, in villages. He continued the frescos at the Palacio Nacional, developed projects, scenographies, jottings... you name it! It was like an antediluvian waterfall, that enormous fountain that emerges from the cracks of creation, a mastodontism of paint.

Suddenly, the giant swayed. The logical breakdown arrived, the first cancerous manifestations. He said nothing, just went on working. Nevertheless, he made a trip to the Soviet Union, seeking a cure. In the USSR he was overwhelmed by tributes and brought back with him a new exposition, which he exhibited successfully in his own home. He declared that he had been cured and that he had never felt better. On December 8, 1956, he celebrated his seventieth birthday, and his admirers proclaimed him "the greatest genius in contemporary plastic art." There was a popular gathering in front of his "Pedregal Pyramid" [the place where he lived and worked, —Tran.], and people brought flowers and song. Children, old folks, workers, professionals from all disciplines, came to congratulate him. In the middle of the twentieth century, people climbed up and down the stone steps of that imitation of an Aztec temple. It was exciting. It looked as if all the demiurges of the Mexican Valley had made a date to meet at that place. The museum-pyramid of Rivera, located in the *Pedregal of San Pablo Tlepetlapa,* is a monumental structure of vast proportions, an actual materialization of Rivera's spirit. The ground floor is dark; one wanders through it as in restless dreams, those dreams that tell us things we can't remember but feel afterwards. The palaces of the princes of the Anahuac must have been like this, colossal, depressing, full of a threatening, rocky solidity. But as one goes up to the floors above, one receives the consolation of light and, witnessing the smiling landscape, a confrontation with limitless beauty.

Everywhere, from corbels and niches craftily located, the visitor is faced by the horrendous visages of ancient deities. One touches with one's eyes the huge past in a magical act of extreme simplicity.

Today that sumptuous tomb, that Mexican *Gizeh* is empty, as if without substance. It contains more than 40,000 sculptures, but it is missing its key treasure: the body of Diego Rivera. It is a castle without ghosts, a legend without the dead; something unimaginable because it doesn't project a shadow. But the day will come when, from the Rotunda of Illustrious Men (where municipal pride deposited his remains) the great artist will be moved to the atrium where he definitely belongs by his own right. The residential neighborhood of the illustrious has residents like Amado Nervo, and complications could arise. On the other hand, in the pyramid of *Tlepetapa,* the remains of Rivera could rest beside his beloved shadows.

• • •

On the 12th of August, 1949, I headed for the Villa of San Angelín, a few kilometers from Mexico City, where Diego had his studio. The object was to interview him on the basis of his Exposition at the Palace of Bellas Artes.

I lost most of the day. Rivera showed up late and had to deal with several people who had arrived before me. Most were tourists, the kind that touch his hands and prove to themselves that geniuses still exist.

I wanted to talk with him face to face, to observe him and obtain a private sense of his personality. I hadn't made any concrete plans, not even formulated a special set of questions since experience had taught me that an initial contact involving a spontaneous chat can yield the most faithful impression of an individual.

On the way to San Angelín it occurred to me to ask Rivera the simplest things, the most humble, that which being known is ignored. Like, "What is a painter?" "What is a painting?" and "How do you make a mural?" It hadn't occurred to anyone, facing Rivera, to technically take advantage of that childish restlessness when a child arrives at that tremendous age of "why this, why that."

"Father, what is a car?" "What are trees made of?"

Really, the matter was settled. I would interview Rivera about the most fascinating issues of the craft with the greatest simplicity. I would face the monster in his own labyrinth and stretching my hand past the bars of his intimacy, ask him for the facts of his life.

On the way there, I decided to wander about a while around his castle, that Aztec castle where one feels and senses the palpitating heart of the past. The studio-home of Rivera, intact at this date, is different from the other buildings in the area. To the right are the servants' quarters, and to the left the three-story studio connected to the main building by a cement bridge. On the top floor is a workroom reached by an outdoor stairway. In front, making do as a barrier, is a row of cacti, the representative plant of Mexico.

Rivera's studio presented the typical disorder of an artist's dwelling, but all working materials were in their place, most carefully guarded by Manuel, his faithful servant.

In a corner of the room one could see a shelf with pre-Hispanic sculptures, but the best of the priceless, 30,000-piece collection was on the first floor, from where they were transported to the pyramid at the Pedregal, where he planned to be interred with his treasures, like the famous pharaohs of Thebes.

For years, Rivera invested large amounts of money collecting pre-Hispanic pieces and he had at his service an army of Indians in charge of finding him monoliths or Aztec deities from anywhere in the republic. He was the most conspicuous visitor of tombs in America; his nails were black with earth thousands of years old.

The study had little furniture, but in his private rooms he had an astonishing collection of highly colorful silk shawls, which he used on his models when he was ready to paint them. Also to be found there were stuffed birds, Andean and Tibetan caps, stone pipes, and musical instruments. But the things that caught a visitor's attention the most were the Judases, colossal dolls made from cardboard and sticks created by anonymous artists, to be burned after Easter. Among these figures were also devils to be found; and Death herself, the perennial beloved of the Mexican people, who used to adorn pre-Hispanic temples thousands of years ago. Rivera loved these products of popular art passionately.

In this room we are describing, so well protected from street noises, the painter would work twelve to fourteen hours daily. There he painted naked women, African blacks, famous artists, indigents and beggars. Clara Bow and Paulette Goddard posed there for hours. The man who was then Treasury Minister, Ramón Beteta, the Canadian poet Phileas Lalane, Mrs. Rubenstein, the Mexican movie star María Féliz, they all sacrificed whole days of immobility just to be painted by Rivera. No one forgets to this day the scandal provoked by the painting of the poet Guadalupe Amor, of Mexico City, when she appeared on canvas totally naked in a local gallery.

When the artist was at work, only people he trusted could gain entrance to his inner sanctum. He would admonish his servants severely if they allowed someone in not previously announced, or anyone he didn't know. I saw government functionaries, professors and American students waiting for hours without being received by the San Angelín dictator.

At eight p.m. the night of August 12, a slow, heavy-set, parsimonious Diego came in to where I was, speaking his Guanajuato version of English and kissing women's hands. I was able to explain my idea to him and he was immediately interested. He invited me into his studio, and while taking off his jacket, said, "Ask me..."

And I asked one, two, twenty… I don't know how many questions 'til the small hours of the night, with him answering from memory, with an incredible accuracy, without pausing, without worrying much about what he might be saying, all of it spilling out in an unconscious and magical manner.

Since the material I obtained was so abundant, the next day I decided to divide the interview into three parts for the newspaper *El Nacional*, where I was a collaborator. I was finishing the third and last part, when the Satan of journalists tempted me. Rivera was able to talk without respite for weeks and weeks on end on life issues, his art, the violent and passionate world in which he lived. Why not take advantage of that mental machine, so full of delicious sound bites, beautiful, human, including contradictory notions of atheism and ferocity? Darkness and lightning bolts inhabited his soul, larger than life passions, thick as jungle vines, tenderness, unconformities and revelations. All that besides his work, his gigantic achievements…. Wasn't this divine liar one of the most interesting artists on the continent, not to mention the many scandals accompanying what he did? Didn't he practice the art of lying in an exquisite manner never heard of before? Weren't his cape and sword scandal itself, his political radicalism and his demon the flame of the savage past? All of this meant that I had to arm myself with patience.

I got in touch with him by phone, telling him that I wanted to continue our chats, and he agreed. He was delighted to accept, of course, because now he'd have a loudspeaker to propagate his views, unburden himself, criticize, theorize, and unwrap before a sharp mirror his life as an artist, so intense and vital that today, even as a dweller of the night, he casts no shadow.

This is the way my newspaperman's task began, one I thought would last one day and ended up taking fifty-two weeks; each

Sunday for a whole year. *El Nacional* kept publishing everything and when Rivera was out of town I'd make the interview up, at my own risk, talking *at* him.

I wrote the articles at all hours, in different places and ways: in cabarets, at my desk, in busses, up on scaffoldings, in private cars and taxis, using pencils, pens, typewriters, telephones and television. Rivera would dictate without moderation, vertiginously, without pausing, sometimes without breathing. Other times he'd dictate reluctantly. My job at such a time was limited to placing my hands on a little table without nails and invoking the spirit. The table would move and I would interpret its movements. The development of the talks was my own, all questions were my inspiration. I'd present him with specious questions to trip him up and have him reveal some invaluable confidence. But I would do it with respect for his person and admiration for his genius.

All this with the joyful anticipation of someone beneath an apple tree, waiting for the fruit to fall in bunches, for whole sentences would come from his mouth one after the other, and I would have to grab them as they went by. What a way to speak! Without the least sense of what a limit might be, or a pause. He loved his notions and would speak like a deranged orator, like a medium, like an oppressive loudspeaker spewing its propaganda. But what a difference between a logomaniac without sense and this precious disorder of the aesthetic lover, of a Rivera presenting himself! I had to write down his words with idiomatic mendacity, jotting down theories, observations, and the names of foreign personages and artists whose correct spelling would cause endless problems. When transcribing my notes I would be in serious trouble until I could take refuge in encyclopedias and reference books.

Rivera appears in my texts like a storm of leaves.

Every word in this book is a footprint of his enormous vocal leaps, footprints he pressed against my ears like someone stepping on wet cement. I have gathered them, heavy, rough, poorly schooled and profound, the footprints of a fat man who doesn't equivocate. The soles of his shoes had nails but I never saw myself as a rug. I have respected the raging of this centaur ready for a fight, the invectives out of place, his venting, the tremendous guffaw of his irony. Had I suppressed those aspects, ignitions of his nature, I'd be presenting a false Rivera, a Rivera subject to the conventional. That would be a crime against fidelity.

Nor have I had to rearrange the style too much, convinced that the task of an interview is to retain the energy of a conversation. These pages obey the speed of lips, so to speak, with the need to finish before a deadline. Perhaps the paragraphs filling these pages capture eternal moments, sketching his temperament more accurately than careful and overworked treatments.

Many people will like this basic way of presenting Diego Rivera, but others will inevitably feel the words of the artist as a sudden sting, like the hives produced by certain shellfish. I am sure they will feel a need to refuse the violence used, a desire to argue with his notions directly. Unfortunately, Rivera is incapable of replying personally. Only his work remains, and in it, forever shining, is the testimony of his human truth.

1

AT THE FOOT OF THE FOUNTAIN

What is a painter?

A painter is, just as any artist, the product of the society in which he lives; individually, a being possessing a neuro-glandular system and an ocular apparatus that aids him in his work, agents that are nothing but receptive conductors, transmitting apparatuses for the aspirations, desires and struggles of the masses that intervene in the medium produced.

What is a picture?

A surface, level or not, covered by colors that determine forms and volumes in space.

And what is a color?

A vibration that affects the photoelectric cells of the retina in a particular way and transmits it to the brain, which then passes it to the endocrine-sympathetic system producing repercussions in accordance with the nature of the vibration, and finally exciting glandular secretions.

What is propaganda art?

All art is propaganda. Sometimes its content reveals the kind of message involved. In other cases, it is veiled ingeniously. *The Crucifixion* by Mathias Grünewald is propaganda for the devout Christian; the lovers of cardinals playing the role of virgins or saints was propaganda to the taste and liking of papal power, or the *Still Life* by Chardin, showing a slice of bread, a bottle of wine, a plate of food and a knife, was propaganda for the French Revolution, which called bread bread and wine wine, contrary to the chromes of the Rococo period showing the whoring duchesses and the gigolo dandies as nymphs and satyrs. Any battle painting is propaganda in favor of what was lost. Each Venetian painting depicting a moonlit night with a handsome gondolier rowing lovers is propaganda for the whorehouses of this earth. It doesn't matter how abstract a painting is. From Kandinsky on, to the last of his followers, it has all been propaganda. Those who maintain to be of no party, and who are quick to sell their work to left-wing, center or right-wing buyers, with no problem or inconvenience, practice the most open of propagandas, the most political, the most opportunistic and abject of them.

Should art be political?

Art should be nothing but art, but there is not a single activity, including prayer and love, that isn't essentially political. It's not for nothing that Aristotle defined man, with marvelous clarity and precision, as a political animal. In our time the definition gets inverted, but changing the factors doesn't alter the result.

How is a mural painted?

You choose the wall, or take what is offered without a choice in the matter. You conceive what you are going to paint and, if you are a muralist, you continue the work of the architect, bearing in mind the circumstances that condition the location, objectively and subjectively. If you are not a muralist, you pay no attention to such factors. In both cases, the surface of the wall is covered as if it were the canvas of a picture, producing forms and volumes in space.

What do you seek in a portrait, the anecdote or the concept?

The anecdote helps me fix the attention on a moment in the existence of the subject, and once this is fixed, to reach the plasticity of the concept.

In what part of the face lies the secret of its expression?

The secret depends on the relation of the whole to its parts, and it is precisely the right expression of these relations and their own characteristics that make the portrait the supreme objective of the art of painting, since it becomes the relatively fixed image of a human existence thanks to the work of another human being.

Do you paint what you think or what you see?

I can't paint without seeing or thinking, therefore I think depending on what I see and paint what I see and think. When previously unseen forms are painted, they have been thought-of beforehand. The plastic characteristics of a painting conceived in that fashion depend on whether they have been seen in the palette or on the canvas. We then modify those forms, quantities, qualities and specific relations according to our sensibilities.

What is cubism?

Cubism is the art of not placing the chamber pot on the dining room table.

And expressionism?

Expressionism can only be defined by German critics prior to the war.

Impressionism?

According to master Manet's definition, it means to paint the way a bird sings.

How do you feel about the Aztec Codices?

In a passionate way. My drawings resemble the codices the way a prickly pear resembles another prickly pear because they are the fruit of the same Mexican cactus plant.

What was your impression when you got to know the Bonampak *murals?*

I naively confess that I felt a great emotion and a vague fear when I saw them in photographs and reproductions, especially the battle scene, because it really looked as if I had done them one day when I surely painted better than I do now. Then I laughed at myself since we are mathematically the same and I am just one of the many that painted *Bonampak*, and who will continue while Mexico is Mexico and we love it with all and each of the cells of our organisms.

Who are the best critics?

Those whose interests are affected vitally by the form and content of a work of art.

How much money do you have?

Generally, the last amount I have been paid and haven't spent. Frequently, zero pesos, zero cents, because I always have much more I want to spend than money to do it.

If you are an artist of the people, why do you paint the portraits of bourgeois women?

Because there is nothing I love more in this life than a good-looking woman, and fortunately, beauty comes with different characteristics according to social class. If someone accuses me of making circumstantial portraits for tourists, he can go to the devil. Indian themes acquire greater depth for me because I love them the most.

What is man's origin?

Man's origin is the first inter-relative function outside space, measurable in earthly energy and matter; we may add that matter is invariably a form of energy. Consequently, the mind, horrified by this obvious simplicity, has designated this energy-matter complex (that necessary and eternal atom of Epicurus) with the most extravagant names, for example: God.

In which way is Indian romanticism healthy?

Master Dario said it already: "Who is it that isn't a romantic?" In the first place, what is Indian constitutes the only beauty produced by the location where it is born. Consequently, it is superior intrinsically and extrinsically to any subsequent product. The half-breed and the white in America are not a happy biological product. Everything in America that is valuable and significant is rooted in the Indian world, and just as the work of giant types like Walt Whitman, Mexican painting needs to be called giant. When it comes to that which doesn't contain an indigenous basis, Mr. Papini was right: if you could show me a single Latin or Hispanic-American that is essentially original, I would go barefoot on a pilgrimage to ask forgiveness from the Virgin of Guadalupe. It should be well understood that by its own abstract characteristics, the poetic emotion can't be localized in the soil that produces it, even when I can find works here of as high a quality as anywhere else in the world. For us, without the Indian component, it wouldn't be possible to be original. America is a composite of voices emitted by our Jewish forefathers when they discovered the Antillean coasts after a time of navigating terrors. It is also a Toltec term (amerika) that means "country with mountains in its center." That's exactly what our continent is like. As a consequence of that (or without a romantic consequence), in these lands all that which isn't by its root and base indigenous, and which doesn't project itself in time as a national kind of indigenous nature, embracing past, present, and future, will lack life and is of no value.

What is art for?

Art is meant to produce in a human being an aesthetic emotion, a unique phenomenon due to the proper and complete provocation that, passing through the neuro-sympathetic system, moves its adjacent glands so that these may yield their secretions to the organism. This is as necessary to life as those products that feed the digestive system. In consequence, if art is not made, there is a danger of death.

Why are retablos *so vital?*

Because being paintings by the people and for the people, the folk condense in them what remains of their past genius and all that it can be with what remains.

Your concept of Mexican music?

The only Mexican music is that made using the *teponaxtli*, the *huéhuetl*, the *tlapanhuéhuetl*, the *kena*, the percussive gourds, etc. when Mexicans use them. Mexican music is also the transposition of a pre-Hispanic musical core into the present day, meaning the works of Carlos Chavez, not only his marvelous *Sinfonía India*, not only his *H.P. [Horse-Power: Ballet Symphony, —edit.]*, but also his more classical works where he arrives at a purity equal to the palaces of *Mitla*. Chavez is one of the most ignored Mexicans due to the fact that, as has invariably happened throughout the history of art, those artists who express the life of humankind most completely and profoundly, go through a period when those same masses reject them, sometimes violently, and come to hate the essential and superior image of themselves contained in that art, which is, after all, their very expression. Sometimes people are frightened, or offended, before the real and true image of themselves which art has uncovered. That is why there are so many people who not only reject Chavez' value as a creator, but refuse to recognize his role as one of the great builders of our contemporary culture. Neither do I undervalue other artists in close historical proximity to Chavez: men such as Silvestre Revueltas and Blas Galindo. I dearly love their music. Their work is flesh of the flesh, bones of the bones and nerves of the nerves of our Mexican painting, since one could not exist without the others.

And your concept of Mexican architecture?

Mexican architecture ended in the last days of the pre-Hispanic world (architecture, by the way, which one shouldn't call Mexican but *Anahuatlaca*; in other words, American). We could say that it survived potentially in rural homes and in huts of elemental though perfect beauty, and which saw a geographic resurgence conquering the entire globe, as architects of Central Europe stated when gathered in Berlin in 1928. Fortunately today, after the lamentable grotesqueries threatening to convert our city into one of the most horrible on earth with that vulgarity, pretentiousness and ugliness comparable only with San Antonio, Texas, or pseudo-Arizona, a new generation of young architects is coming up showing evident talent, some of them true geniuses. They continue cultivating in Mexico the seeds that the giant of the north throws at us by the fistful, but using our own modality.

What is your concept of Mexican sculpture?

There is a man who began sculpting when he was 52 years old and a porter and cook at the School of Painting in the open air in *Coyoacan*, after rising from peonage to managing a hacienda. At 72 he had realized ten magnificent sculptures. That man can be assumed to be the only such affirmation to come from that weird desert that droughts and floods had brought, precisely where for over two thousand years the greatest sculpture in the world had been made. Today, he is an extraordinary individual, a good medical doctor, curing children and workers without charge. He had begun in obscurity to simply make sculptures, which, in their plastic value, are neither better nor worse than what was made thousands of years ago. Seeing his work we are aware that they are the same since *Anahuac* continues to exist. Their natural contents are not the cosmology of the *Popol Vuh*, but the dialectic material of Marx, Engels and Joseph Stalin. The name of that sculptor is Francisco Arturo Marín. All that is needed is the example of a generative germ from our soil for the entire territory to be covered by similar items. There are bright youth from whom we can expect a renaissance of our sculpture.

What about Mexican poetry?

I like the songs of *Netzahualcóyotl*, the lyrics of indigenous songs that have survived, the mestizo poems of Ramón López Velarde and the very Mexican poetry of the great word-painter Carlos Pellicer. I also like the poetry of that genius, Guadalupe Amor.

Can you give us a key thought that biographers and historians of the future can quote from this work, since you yourself will have chosen it to encompass your life?

I could adopt the motto of Charles of Bourbon: "I had no need of hope to begin with, nor of success to persevere."

How was your childhood?

My childhood was that of a child without a childhood.

What about your awakening, your youth, your first amazement?

From the age of three to six years, I drew machines and battles. Most times I'd invent the first mentioned, not as an image for the sake of the image, but as an expression of the actual object I had devised. I would draw imaginary battles based on the tales my father told of his campaigns against the French intervention and Empire. For a long time I refused to draw mountains in spite of the fact that I lived surrounded by them in Guanajuato, the reason being that I didn't know them from within.

Asked by my father why I didn't draw them, I explained the reason and he patiently took me to visit as many mines as he could. I was fascinated, and full of excitement, I went down using the winches, walking the galleries, bumping into rocks with my feet. After that experience the locomotives I drew at five years of age went across bridges and through tunnels while the soldiers of my battles fought above them.

That same need made me fall madly in love with mechanical toys. There was only one store where they were sold, and it is still there in Guanajuato. The Flower Castle sold candy, pastries, and toys. The proprietor then was a Frenchman, don Enrique Regnie, who had come to Mexico as a conscript among many of the invading armies. He was my father's friend and I was the rapt audience to the accounts of their campaigns. Each time he received a new toy to sell, he would place it strategically in a showcase in the window and I, who was forever checking the store, would catch sight of the novelty and, if I liked it (I only went for machines), I would begin to court the toy as if it were a girl; I'd feel feverish and would blush as I went back and forth in front of that case, glancing sideways at it. Then I would look at it for hours until I could declare my love. I'd march into The Flower Castle and, without any compunction, I would summarily order don Enrique: "Have this sent to my house and jot it down on my father's account."

I would caress the toy with the same sensuality I'd use with my nana Antonia's breasts, or my mother's, years after I had stopped nursing. Then I would try to make it work, and as soon as I knew clearly how it functioned, I'd take it apart to get to know its guts—as with the mountains— and put it together again sure of myself. Sometimes the toy was destroyed, something that has happened to my life many times.

I was proud to have invented a locomotive that didn't resemble any other I had seen. It had a conic boiler placed on a platform ending at the chimney's cylinder, with the fire beneath. The steam would activate a vertical piston on the platform that would directly move the back wheels.

An uncountable number of years later, in New York, Nelson Rockefeller, to whom I had told that childhood memory, invited me to lunch with some engineers and architects at Rockefeller Center and the Transportation Club. The lunch was being served in a private room. Well, in the middle of a table with photos of all kinds on machines, was something I couldn't believe: a large picture of a locomotive from some Pennsylvania mine functioning as I had envisioned one when I was four years of age. People in Guanajuato used to call me "the engineer," but now I don't deal with mechanics, I don't think they were wrong since it is only possible to be a painter, a sculptor, or an architect if you are a plastic engineer; in other words, someone who understands the nature and functioning of the materials he handles.

Among the mechanical toys at the Flower Castle, one day I discovered a doll that impressed me in a new way. It was very large, more or less the size of a girl my age, and I noticed that it resembled one of the girls I knew, Virginia Mena. Instead of playing dumb in front of the case, one Sunday I decided to have her come with me to see the doll, my head abuzz, trying to figure out how I would manage to take the doll apart, get to know its mechanism, and put her back together again. I recall that on the way I felt strange, and that frightened me at first.

In that state, I arrived at her house. I was wearing new shoes and made sure they made a noise on the pavement. I really felt as if my blood was boiling, that it would burst out in a stream from my ears. I arrived at her door after making a lot of noise as I walked. She happened to be in their downstairs hallway, all dolled up in a white embroidered dress with a cobalt blue underpinning. Like the doll, her curls fell on her shoulders. The dress revealed her neck, chest and arms. I felt something I had never experienced before as my eyes surveyed her down to her calves. Her ankles made me understand right away how important such things were. Her feet were tiny and were encased in bejeweled shoes. My blood was surging like the tide, as if it were the river that overran the town at times of floods. As I stood at the entrance, I don't know what gesture she made, what moves; the fact is that when she saw me, Virginia opened her eyes wide, raised her arms, and let out a tremendous scream. That scream resonated within my skull. I couldn't help it, I fell to the floor senseless.

What happened then?

Much later I woke up at home, where Melesio, the hired hand who always followed me everywhere at a distance without interfering, had taken me. Next to my bed was my mother, repeating nothing but "God help me, God help me," and shaking her head. My great aunt was there also, peeking at me sadly without saying a word; my father too, with that friendly expression he reserved for me. He found some pretext to get rid of my mom and great aunt and when we were alone, he had a big smile on his face. He pulled my ear and all he said was, "Gosh, you pug-nosed devil, you sure had the hots for her!"

This whole thing took place days before my birthday party when not only would I be five years old, but I had already learned on my own how to read and write, so strong was my tremendous passion to find out what books had to say.

That day, a worried look on my face, Father said to me, "Don't go thinking I didn't want you to have a good time today. I went early to the Menas and asked the colonel to bring Virginia to you, but unfortunately, the whole family had gone off to their hacienda."

His words made me feel a mixture of satisfaction and humiliation; all I could hold onto was that I had lost my senses in the desire to possess Virginia. So I answered my father angrily, "Why are you involved in what's not your business? If I had wanted to, I would have gotten the doll; you've never known before about my asking them to send toys over. Now I want neither toys nor Virginia." Furious, I stomped the floor with my foot while making fists and repeating, "Do you get it? I don't want toys or Virginia now!"

Father didn't lose his cool. He assumed an extremely affable look and said, "Good, good, wait a minute. He went to his room and came back carrying a gorgeous revolver, enameled in nickel, its handle mother-of-pearl. He also brought a basket full of ammunition, and he said, "Here's your birthday present for this year; I didn't want to give it to you so soon, but it's better that you familiarize yourself with the gun before you have an accident with it. Learn how to handle it right away. It's not beside the point to say that it can be used as a show-piece in front of those buddies of yours, your newly acquired friends, the Mejia Mora girls." He broke off with a hearty laugh while he pulled at one of my ears, adding, "Those gals don't scream like Virginia when you come near them, eh?"

I suppose that my father was either giving me more credit than I was due or, in his great wisdom, was choosing to push me forward so that I could fulfill soon what, one day or another, had to happen. Besides, what my new friends were all about was absolutely correct. The Mejia girls were marvelous then. In those days, miners had their pockets full of pesos by the weekend; those girls nailed a gold coin to the bone tips of their boots, which hugged their ankles and calves like a glove. The sound they made each time one of those stupendous gals paraded her infinite charms over the cobblestone streets and alleys of Guanajuato was precious.

Their hair was exceedingly black, loose or braided, reaching down to their waistlines. And that hair never lacked for a flower. They wore aggressive ones that came down their ears and reached the corner of their mouths with their scorpion-like tendrils. They painted great scars on their cheeks, and their blouses, skirts, and shawls stood out with their bright colors. Since then, I adore cobalt blues, cadmium yellows, and the strong red Indians call *tlapalli*. I also go for the odor of perfumed water and gross, inexpensive perfumes.

I got to be six years old in this manner, at which time I made a speech from the main altar of the Church of San Diego against the collectors of tithes, privileges, and alms (I have told his story many times and everyone thinks it's a lie, but my friend, Mrs. Amalia Caballero de Castillo Ledón checked its veracity scientifically when she stayed in Guanajuato attending a conference on history). I recall other happenings, among them having executed a pencil drawing of a beloved lady when I was twelve years old, studying under don Andrés Ríos. This surprised all my teachers and earned me a stipend of twenty pesos a month, turning me into a careless student and a rake.

I was a pretty boy who learned the philosophy of life under an admirable teacher nicknamed The Baby from Begoña, an undefeatable ball player. He taught me how the most popular Lady of the Theatre, adored by all, from the president of the republic down to the humblest shoeshine boy, including a multimillionaire, was in a position to accept gifts. Because of all this I can assure you I grew up a child without a childhood, if you call childhood that false life in limbo that the criminal stupidity of adults forces minors to endure.

"Nobody ignores," as Wenziner has said, "that Diego Rivera was an exceptionally precocious child."

This precociousness, as we've seen, manifested itself from the age of five, solidifying itself subsequently into a powerful visual memory. Rivera could recall faces and colors from seventy years back, and enjoyed evoking an infancy fully awakened to nature.

What was your first concrete memory, I asked him as we continued talking about his childhood. He answered quickly.

My first concrete, emotional, and plastic memory is of a dog's head larger in size than what we are used to in sculpture these days; a farmer gave it to my father during one of his trips as inspector of schools in the state of Guanajuato. Father had it placed in the small fountain in our yard so that the water came out the dog's snout. That's one of my precise memories and, though it might seem strange, I was just a year-and-a-half old. But from then on I was fascinated by pre-Hispanic sculpture.

Violent, rude, and gross as he was, deep down Rivera had the tenderness of a child. He loved little ones and all manner of plants just as he hated the negative aspects of life. I saw him get rid of a man who suggested he soften his political notions with the worst insults, and days later have tears in his eyes before a sick boy.

Children are always there in his work, you can see them everywhere, constituting a leitmotiv in the paintings, even in those whose subject matter doesn't call for the presence of a delicate being, as in the murals. "We have found," wrote Xavier Villaurrutia, "in this painter of colossal figures, the ingeniousness and tenderness of infancy." That same author went on to compare Rivera with a modern St. Christopher protecting the tender figure of a child.

So, when I asked him why an adult artist finds paintings done by children interesting, he put me through a scientific explanation of that enthralling mystery, so full of planetary verities, where a man can ascertain the artifice of the intellect and sense a primordial freshness.

A smiling Rivera, in that very Mexican way he has to state his notions, unworried and tenderly fierce, replied: "You've hit the mother lode, my dear Cardona!" Then, while he worked on the beautiful portrait of a woman, answered the phone, and received contingents of workers, he went on talking to me:

Children's paintings are not just important, they are extraordinarily important, not only to an artist, but for anyone interested in the development of the human intellect, since what a child paints is a true ideogram showing, with the precision of an X-ray, the defining characteristics of that development for each individual, as well as its connection with the general characteristics of each stage of growth.

A child repeats in his art the shift of matter in its efforts to organize itself, from the mineral level aiming to become a living cell, up to the human vertebra, in a certain way analogous to that of someone subjected to an insulin shock who then passes, as he regains consciousness and is provided with sugar, through the entire zoological stages, managing at first movements similar to those of mollusks, then those of fish, batrachians and simians, then through other vertebrate forms until he recovers his human characteristics. This passage through the evolution of the species clears the subject, so to speak, of the causes that determined his madness, returning him to the condition of a normally-functioning human being.

In that same way, the child, continuing the succession of stages begun with the single cell in that matrix, goes beyond it to express what I call "memories of the species," recalling in the initial tangle of his creative movements, the representation he intends: first a ball. Then that same ball with a hint of eyes, mouth, and nose, to which are later added, emerging from it, two lines aiming to represent arms, then arms and legs. Finally, another ball is added to the primitive one so that neck, trunk, etc. appear in a more or less literal image of what he wants to represent, dominated, with lesser intensity, by the concept that first guided his movements, and that to be substituted by a new concept stemming from observations of the real object of its true features, each time sharper and more complex, until we have its life in the contemporary physical world.

The effort to recognize our physical world, and the nature of the concept that the child forms of that world before he paints anything (a concept freer than that of the adult), means that children's art is of enormous value for the artist. For him, it has the same value as that of an insulin or adrenalin shot that produces the shock, the run through the stages previously mentioned, so as to arrive through these means at the unconscious and subconscious; a trip that brings back the memory of the species, arriving at his own, free from the psychological traumas that in so many ways prevail as preconceptions over actual circumstances, forcing man to live a life of disparity with the reality of the physical world he inhabits, and which constitutes the phenomenon we call madness.

So, children's paintings, fruit of concepts freer than those of adults, can serve to bring back to reason artists gone crazy with concepts and prejudices of their own and of others. That's the great value of children's paintings, which we could well call therapeutic for adult artists, and not just for them, but for all human beings whose historic-social consciousnesses have clouded their initial perceptive and conceptual faculties. In other words, children's art, well presented, has the value of being an incredibly important hygienic mental and social medium. The pure, high aesthetic emotion that children's art is apt to produce is an integral component for the hygiene we suggest.

I was surprised by this reply and wanted to bring Rivera back to continue the argument by focusing on primitive art as separate from children's art. We know that this last corresponds to the world of virginal conscience while primitive art is adult and wise. But a false appreciation of plastic values tries to establish a dangerous connection between them, producing a confusion that obscures the organizing vision of both phenomena. Nevertheless, though we express it that way, the work of children and primitivism have certain elements in common, merging them precisely where they hide their actual created jewels: in the absence of malice or, as Rivera puts it, preconceptions and prejudices. This aspect of our conversations has a surprising educational value involving his precious elementary nature. That was my intention in formulating my question in this manner:

Are the characteristics of so-called primitive art as easy to assimilate as those of children's art?

We have to understand one another on the concept of primitive art. We hear called primitive the art of the men who executed wonderful sculpture-like paintings in the caverns of Dordogne and Altamira, who lived during prehistory, while we also hear called primitive, artists who lived eight or ten years before Christ, as well as others who flowered in the VIII, the XIII, and even the XV century of the Christian era. Because of that, we are obligated to conclude that people qualify art as primitive, not due to the antiquity of its production as relates to the age of the world and of mankind, but due to certain characteristics that appear to be produced at any time in history in relation to those aspects of art as it evolves in time.

Recognizing this, then, we observe an extremely curious happening, and that is that what is called primitive invariably contains a larger dose of genuine observation than that employed in epochs not considered primitive, quite the opposite; times of sophisticated artistic activity, are qualified, not by the same growth in culture or society, but precisely by their decay. That is the only area where we can relate children's art with that of the adult we denominate primitive, since both periods of production are distinguished by concepts emerging from a freer observation than that of preconceptions and prejudices.

For example, if we call primitive the art of the cave man, this is only an admission in terms of human time and not of the intrinsic plastic values that characterize it, reaching a maximum excellence not only aesthetically but scientifically; and not only not superseded but not even equaled in subsequent times. Cave art expresses exactly all truths regarding movement and form insuperably represented there. When modern man produces photographic images with machines and chemical compounds that act with the incredible speed in thousands and ten thousands of a second, such methods confirm the exactitude and truth found in the representation of the movements of living beings made by cave men. The attribution of the term primitive to such art is ridiculous. On the other hand, in sophisticated times of realistic pretension, we discover the falseness of all those concepts serving to validate plastic art.

2

THE AESTHETIC OF THE VALLEY OF MEXICO

Let's look now at the Valley of Mexico with Rivera's help. This is a prodigious valley, and innately connected with it, self-begotten, establishing a mimesis truly magical, we encounter the Mexican master José María Velasco (1840-1912), an optic genius. Velasco's importance is so great that when I asked Rivera about the value of the valley as a source for landscapes, he replied, "The Valley of Mexico is, in its physical reality, parallel to the plastic realities of the marvelous paintings by Velasco."

I insisted, asking if Velasco had any precedents, and Rivera, without looking at me, but moving a few steps back to check his last stroke on the painting he was doing, said, "Velasco doesn't have anyone before or after him."

Do you believe, given the extraordinary fidelity to render vast distances that the master had, and his amazing grasp of atmospheric values, that he possessed different or abnormal optic capabilities than the rest of humankind?

When my teacher Velasco painted his final renditions of the valley (by the way, the most marvelous of all), he was already using glasses. On the other hand, it is completely impossible to find one single point of view in the actual landscapes to correspond or even come close to the composition of his paintings. The poet Carlos Pellicer and several young devotees of Velasco, traveled all over the valley attempting to locate those points of view without even finding a single one that would correlate with them, all of which proves that Velasco's paintings owe more to a plastic concept, a scientific awareness of the structure of the world, than to a photographic vision of it. Don José María Velasco was, without question, a learned man when it came to geology and natural history. He had such a grasp of the earth's history that he was able to reinterpret it logically to serve the plastic needs of his work.

The volcanic cones, hills, and plains in Velasco's paintings could, speaking with rigorous geologic logic, remain where they are in his pictures, but they are never to be found in the place corresponding to their geographic reality. Each time he painted a picture, don José María Velasco would rebuild the Valley of Mexico. At the same time, he was a learned man in both geology and botany (author of the best treatise on the flora of the valley, which has yet to be published) and a physicist extraordinarily ahead in relation to the level of that science at that time.

He understood all color phenomena, all formal relationships. He was truly an epic poet in charge of a new metaphor: science. Besides all his knowledge pertaining to natural matters, he was a marvelous geometrician in the full sense of that word, a master of space achievable through mathematical means. Thanks to perspective, geometry, and the trigonometry of space, he could not only surmise things, but used precise formulas to deal with spherical forms of space with all the consequences that relativity brings with it. If some day we can overcome the apathy and imbecility in which we are drowning, Velasco's papers relating to what we are discussing will be published and specialists will be able to confirm my words.

Velasco was able to create a true geometry of color with his palette (in other words, a scale of tones each conceived thanks to his infinite sensibility and scientific acumen) that allowed him to place each tone at a certain distance from the eye of a viewer, in such a precise way that the viewer finds himself as a matter of fact before real space, parallel to the geographic and physical space that Velasco saw. Thanks to that, whoever looks at his paintings believes he is seeing a precise copy of a certain location; he thinks he is seeing a view, a photo of the real thing when the opposite is precisely what you have, forms and colors perfectly abstract, organized by the creative will of the artist, who in this way arrived at the concrete, a process that leads to a superior kind of realism. Nothing in the history of art, at least not in what we know of it in the five parts of the world, has arrived at the results that Velasco achieved. So it can be said, that given how painting is a language that uses color to express a plastic reality, José María Velasco, a Mexican, is doubtless the best and greatest painter in the world.

He had the elegance to keep his distance from the stupid, the pedants, the insensitive, and the idiots who flood the world of art and letters, having also the supreme elegance of making them believe that in viewing an abstract composition, they were looking at a photograph of the physical world. I can still recall the marvelous laughter of the master aware of this. Nobody has ever laughed better. Many years might have to pass before all this enters the public domain. It won't happen before the destruction of our present society and the building of a new one, but as of now, in this part of the world where it took place, Velasco would be the most popular painter, the most beloved landscape artist of the masses in a socialist country.

It must be said that, since the destruction of the worm-eaten for the sake of a new and healthy world will be carried out for the benefit of the working masses of the world, Velasco is already the most admired and popular artist by the best of the allies of these masses and by the best poets of the continent. Some day, when daylight comes to be the historically correct moment, if his paintings survive the disasters that might occur, don José María Velasco will be the most popular painter in the world, just as the most beloved poet of the people will be Walt Whitman.

What places in the valley are the most important from the point of view of art and archeology?

Objectively speaking, there is no spot in the valley that doesn't qualify. We are tempted to answer that it is *Tlatilco*, but the *Pedregal* would object. And if we accept the two, we have to remember that on the ground and below the ground of the bullfight ring, several elephants appeared simply to testify by their enormous size the smallness and pernicious anemia of the brains of those who had established a ridiculously youthful chronicle for the age of the valley. We must realize that an archeologist with no geology is like a doctor with no anatomy. It so happens that *Tlaltelolco* and *Tenochtitlán* built their foundations in the valley during the greatest periods of culture in the *Anahuac*.

Its hills hide treasures, the surrounding mountains also. Really, for one or another reason, the entire Valley of Mexico is important for archeology and pre-history. If you talk of beauty, there is no corner that doesn't possess it without manifest intensity.

Is there no ugliness in the valley?

No! Ugliness has only been made by the men who have come to dirty it with their presence. Among them, nobody is going to quarrel that the prize goes to the false architects that the valley has had to suffer. Among the places made ugly, the worst is Mexico City, where businessmen who don't understand have destroyed a handsome Spanish city built on the ruins of a marvelous Aztec city, all done to exchange it for that infected abortion of an inferiority complex, the congenital boot-licking of the Mexican *criollo* [the native white, —Trans.] and a large number of the half-breeds, who manage to infect the foreigners who settle here, especially those coming from the Levant, who never lose the mentality of money-lenders and hawkers of ties, stockings and trinkets, and who are the worst plague to have visited us.

Of course, it must be said that this plague could not have taken hold were it not aided by those dandified, audacious and pretentious architects, the accomplices of every thieving or ignorant functionary, every cheating shop owner, every suspicious banker, every stock compiler and exploiter of wartime who has demolished a poor man's shack by blood and fire to erect ugly and uncomfortable housing projects.

These architects are sufficiently idiotic to ignore, and assert it in writing, that academism consists in respect for the correct, patriotic, and aesthetic plastic norms of a country, and not in the repetition of previously-conceived works, no matter how old or new they be. In this way, these dandified bastards feel contemporary and anti-academic, repeating formulas created by master Walter Gropius or Le Corbusier.

They do this in the name of a functioning that has no function, unless that be to construct in the smallest space possible apartments they then rent for as much as possible, or the function that what cooks in the kitchen or is discharged in the toilet perfumes the entire unit, something to admire in every famous individual apartment of theirs.

That is the way it is; these gentlemen and young bucks are all, without exception, repeaters of formulas so academic, so evilly academic, as the duplicators of catalog homes meant for Yankees of bad taste, perpetuating that intestinal style on the outside, fecal inside. They call it, thanks to its decorations, California Colonial, creating the only ugly location in the valley, which is Mexico City, the ugliest neighborhoods on earth being the Lomas de Chapultepec and Chapultepec-Polanco.

In an ideal yet practical reconstruction of the old and new capital, Rivera outlined the dimensions of the city. As the reader will see, it consists of a fantastic project, as are all the genuine experiences of an artist. I had asked him in what way could Mexico City become the most beautiful and interesting city in the world and he showed me, with that fatality needed to calculate clearly and even skimpily "the exaggeration of grandeur" as Zweig said about Balzac's commercial visions "passionately impatient and impatient with passion," how Mexico City could be the leading capital of the world in beauty and comfort, in accordance with the following:

I/ Preserving the reservoirs of *Xaltocan, Zumpango, Texcoco, Chalco,* and *Xochimilco*, which regulated the climate of the valley, where the dryness of the air and the saturation of water vapors producing evaporation, are due to the high altitude of the place. This phenomenon used to clean the air of stuff in suspension at the same time that it avoided those dust storms that make living in the city today intolerable; it also permitted intensive horticulture and floriculture, the cultivation which the Russian Baviloff, the greatest specialist in these matters, called the best in the world. Those reservoirs, besides providing definitive climactic advantages, would give modern Mexico City vacation spots, boating facilities, swimming spots, and so on. Together with the waters of the valley itself, they would make the place enchanting and fertile, while the imbeciles who dried the lakes have not been able to gain a thing from the swamplands they obtained after destroying the source of an immense national asset.

II/ Once the water reservoirs are conserved (in other words, the region made habitable) it would be necessary to preserve the old city, its undeniable beauty. This conservation would bring the inhabitants of the city of palaces a larger annual income than all the present buildings drowning it, (great danes compared to chihuahuas), so extremely expensive to ground in the soil, so inefficient and uncomfortable to boot.

III/ Conserving the Spanish city, we could do what the Austrians did with old Vienna, making it a city for pedestrians full of museums, libraries, schools of advanced learning specializing in history and ethnography; government buildings involving little traffic; and luxurious residences, that kind of luxury that befits the refined local conservative taste, or that of foreigners who with the greatest pleasure and openness, would pay very high prices for a temporary residence in palaces impeccably furnished in style, made for comfort without destroying their original, characteristic beauty. The materials to build these museums are abundant and the cost would be minimal. There is also enough material to build archives and libraries of the highest cultural value. Investors would catch on, after the initial attempts in this direction, to the possibility of luxury residences and hotels. In other words, the conservation of what was built by the Spanish and the locals of good taste, would provide the inhabitants of today's capital with eight hundred to one billion dollars of income annually, if only thanks to foreign visitors.

IV/ The new city should be built on the marvelous circle of hills extending from the Guadalupe Sierra to the foothills of *Ajusco,* including the Pedernal area. Given the nature of the ground, instead of the tremendously expensive cost of foundations in the lower parts of the city, we would require quite light foundations, at less expense, without requiring the vast cutting down of forests to create inefficient lots. Among those hills, commercial zones and cheap housing could be established. That's where large government structures, public hygiene and assistance buildings, and schools could be erected. Everything could be distributed without one thing interfering with another. The inclination of the land would favor drainage and the distribution of water with record one hundred percent efficiency. It would be enough to place the liquid deposits high enough to establish recycling plants to convert the city's discards really and positively into gold, adding to the city's coffers. For this marvelous semi-circle, it would be easy to plan great circulation arteries and the web for local intercommunication.

What such a city could have been like has been shown by the assertions of some architects referring to the zone which is mostly irremediably lost now, as well as by the houses built by young architects of talent. It was possible to have arrived at a really supra-modern, really American style, not only due to the use of traditional forms, but because it would have been organically rooted to the landscape. This has been demonstrated by the visionary gardens and dwellings built by a few valuable architects. Under these conditions involving our kind of architecture, painting, and sculpture, Mexico City would be of such beauty that it would attract residents and visitors from all over the world. Anyone but an idiot will understand this. Anyone that denies all these advantages is an enemy of our country's prosperity, be he a Mexican or a foreigner.

3

POPULAR ART

Mexico has the brightness of singing blood: it is there in its popular arts, most ancient, and noble in origin.

Smooth singing, a spellbound handling of its manual creations, detained miracles in the arms of homeward-bound light. These things are ours in plazas and arcades, by the sides of roads and within those vital forests that are our marketplaces, where shapes like naive diamonds call out to the surprised passerby. What a trove of treasures! Sculptures, silver and lacquered objects, furniture, brilliant textiles, ceramics, and toys of all types ... The popular arts turn Mexico into an immense, bewitching bazaar. Death floats over this store of mirrors, and something suggestive of a racial secret smiles at us through flowers and fresh water. But not all is pure joy. Up to a few years ago, anything created by the people was considered harmful to the interests of boudoir aesthetes, while today this marvelous art has conquered a more or less dignified, more or less just position, leaving it on the margin of humiliation.

Artists exist in the millions, but we will cite just one: don Tito Reyes, who, each January 6th, would bring to the town of Metepec's *plaza, in the state of Mexico, the figurines of Melchior, Gaspar, and Balthazar (Kings, which lent him his own last name). He was an old man of seventy-two. From his person emanated a genetic breath of demiurges and doves. Around 1900 he dedicated himself to work in clay. He made his own casts, chose his paints and never allowed anyone to interfere with his compositions. One day he made three Wise Kings to commemorate the star that guided them. People applauded the figures and from that point on that is what he made, establishing in his village this "buying of the kings" that acquired the status of a yearly rite.*

Half an hour from Toluca, among hamlets and dust storms, Metepec *each Monday reveals the sweat of its work, a grand mixture of objects and colors: throw rugs, vessels, pots, fried food, pyramids of hats, in the midst of the hawking of wares and the silence of herbs. The flatware, preciously glazed, presents its share of corny doves and album phrases, which the sunlight brings out magnificently. The church on its hill dominates the plaza; you can hear the hum and joy of the marketplace from there. We walk down and are lost in the noise. At the first stand, we ask where we can buy don Tito's Kings.*

"Oh, Sir, don Tito has left us!"

"How can that be?"

"He died four days ago, sir!"

The entire town knew of his death. We made two or three more inquiries, with the replies dealing with the start of the new year, the cold, the exhaustion… this on the 6th of January, 1942.

Don Tito's ranch is about one kilometer from the plaza. There, in a miserable reed hut, next to the firing oven, he and his wife worked. His family lives next door, a nephew and his wife, who don Tito initiated into the mysteries of ceramics. When we got there they were putting the last touches on the Kings, but these were different. They explained, "We want to make Kings like those of our uncle but we don't have the molds; these have turned out differently."

At any rate, the family wanted to take them to the plaza to continue the tradition, but death took with it the original spark. Then, something more original came to be. The nephew's Kings came mounted on indefinite-looking animals, a mixture of dogs and horses. Melchior appears mounted on an elephant with mouse ears and a pink snout. The old figures were of one piece and the decoration, the color of the robes and the attitude, the expression on their faces revealed true art. When one considers the so-called workshop and the primitive way the work was made, the impression is even greater.

Diego Rivera went to Metepec *one day, discovered the magic stuff and gave birth to the notoriety of that mine. Since then, Mexican artists have filed through there, purchasing those miraculous toys until, with time, don Tito became a legend, and* Metepec *the cradle of the Three Kings.*

But there is more: besides those three worshipers, the popular artist would wrest from clay a whole fabulous imagery, fruit of dream and magic, things stellar and recondite, where those who understand the subconscious keep finding strange origins: sirens and snakes, animals from the past, lions with moustaches and crowns, roosters and tiny horses of incredible color. The malice of the outsider turned enthusiastic and, in a second, saw how amazed city folk would be, and what the thirst of the tourist could bring.

That is how the pieces began to move, from hand to hand, till in Mexico City, decorators rushed to place them in special shop windows, adding a touch of grace and ingenuity to Juarez Avenue. The metropolis exhibited, next to gold and festival silks, a treasure come from afar. The Indian, great in his blood, was once again able to let the earth show how to break the pride of the city with its fecund humility.

I have wanted to remember these things now that Rivera, speaking about popular art, arrives with me at the world of reminiscences, explaining in his way how it is that the figures of Tito Reyes have the same disposition and technique as those from Colimas and Nayarit which, according to the specialists, date back to 2,400 years ago.

The subject is long and Rivera is in a hurry. As an extraordinary lover of all things Mexican, Rivera answers our questions about popular art as follows:

During the Colonial period and before it was called popular art, it was, as it was afterwards and it is today, the true art of the Mexican people, manifesting itself where it could outside the fashion imposed by the conquerors first, then by their successors, who considered it then and continue to do so today in a more or less shameful way as far as the basic population is concerned, especially in the countryside (and above all in those areas that remain purely Indian) as different from those belonging to the middle, wealthy, or aristocratic class, and who have inherited the mentality of those who divided the population of the country into Indians and 'people of reason.'

Before the Revolution, farmers, workers, and artisans had lived in a world separated from the middle classes by an abyss which became deeper in the period between 1862 and 1902 due to the influence of Europe in both the conservative (monarchical in intent with Maximilian), and the liberal side. Among certain social groups the French influence was greatest, among others the German, and among a small minority that considered itself the most distinguished, the English.

We should remember that Guillermo de Landa y Escandón, an amiable personage who was governor of the Federal District and the great pontiff of the Jockey Club, had a direct cable connection with London so that each morning he could learn what the weather was like in the British capital and dress accordingly. With great discretion, he put up with the heat among us wearing the most elegant clothes meant for the cold at home.

In those days, typical of such types, popular art was ignored completely with the exception of the riding tackle these personages wore to show off when visiting their *pulque* farms.

The people continued creating their own art regardless. It was the only art in Mexico anyway, together with the admirable portraits of Estrada, Bustos, and the painters of the Veracruz school such as José Guadalupe Posada, which were part of the people's art. The immense don José María Velasco, and painters of great distinction, such as Félix Parra and Petronilo Monroy, just as the ignored regionalist, my teacher, don Andrés Ríos, were part of what was happening even though some of their work was academic, and they were professors at the Academy.

We must add that the twenty thousand etchings of Posada were absorbed by the people, who bought millions of his prints, and while admiring them, singing and reading their romances, praying their prayers, learning their own legends and stories.

The original etchings go for high prices today.

When a popular work of art is close to disappearing, its price goes up as an exchange item. Its old samples turn into museum items, always expensive, and what is left of that production is grabbed by intermediaries who, relying on its aesthetic credit, resell at much higher prices than imagined by its creators. They sell them not only to nationals, but to foreigners. Then, and only then, is when intellectuals get interested in the popular arts. This phenomenon began to occur around 1921 when they christened that art with the odious and discriminatory name of folk art so as to deal commercially with the art of the people without cheapening the specialized production by specialists of official art and literature. They assume an amiable and protective attitude towards the work of the folk, wanting the public to understand that this superb art is recognized and survives thanks to the intervention of the experts, when the very opposite is true. This justifies the shameless exploitation of a people's art by businessmen and the industrial bourgeoisie with the complicity of intellectuals who adopt the role of its saviors. This is a typical example of the creative force of a people overwhelmed by a capitalistic bourgeoisie.

The most naïve official specialists rebel furiously against folk art and accuse as traitors to their class those colleagues whose work tends to ally itself with the popular as opposed to the bourgeois-capitalist tradition. You see this peculiar attitude among the best artists who use it to protect their professional class interests, impelled by the most elemental survival instinct. It happens frequently that the drawing of an unknown artist on a piece of popular pottery has a hugely bigger aesthetic value and, in consequence, might be worth more, doing better than the work of professional artists. These, in turn (and perhaps most often unconsciously) manifesting a most definite sense of self-protection, will attack to the death this injection of popular elements into their official art. They do this fearing that the intrinsic worth of artists from the people might raise their plastic values to the proper level, to the detriment of the prices obtained in the market place by these unchallenged artists.

This has happened in Mexico, notably among the most successful and valuable artists. Understanding the situation and changing tactics with brilliant skill, the best-known artist in the world, Pablo Picasso, has anticipated that competition by himself creating popular ceramics with a populist political position. This proves that this Spanish genius has a greater political and, above all, commercial sense than our Mexican geniuses, Orozco, Siqueiros, and others. It is not in vain that Spaniards, be they Francophile or Communist, when they reach America, turn out to be excellent businessmen without losing their intrinsic qualities: just as the great Picasso has naturally not lost his, being the best painter of all these businessmen. When you rob the folk using your genius, the actual result is that the thief becomes part of the people, which, after all, are the only ones that can save the artists of our country.

What is called "popular art" through a series of circumstances is, by and large, an agrarian art. In the countryside and in the small towns, the artisan has a lower standard of living than in the large cities, but disposed with more time to enjoy his own creations. When countries are industrialized in the capitalist mode, the conditions of the peasants involved in creating popular art suffer; their work becomes less available and eventually disappears. This occurs with greater violence in the cities. As Guadalajara has grown, the arts of the folk have degenerated thanks to the bad taste of the bourgeoisie, who have turned their artists into salaried workers, with the complicity of businessmen with even less taste. These people imagine they can improve their sales by destroying the beauties of authentic production, underestimating, and offending the taste of foreigners, whom they disrespectfully call *turistas*, while begging for their dollars, offering everything for sale, including their professional dignity.

This is not an exclusively Mexican phenomenon; other countries suffer the same conditions. One manifestation of this process is the degeneration of architectural styles, and the fact that a whole bunch of ex-functionaries have become hotel owners, with their hotels in worse taste the more Mexican they become, in contrast to foreign owners who employ Mexican architects of worth to conserve the character of the country and utilize, without spoiling it, the authentic production of the people's art.

In which way color comes to dominate form totally in the hands of anonymous artists is what Rivera explains next. Form, primitive and by itself apparent, is absolutely superseded by the sense of color, which, in the hands of the people, reaches a unique brightness. These secrets of elaboration, unconscious on the one hand, reach the 'cultivated' artist, who manages to sell his work for fabulous prices without apparently recalling its humble and yet magical origins, like a butterfly hovering over mud. With tremendous irony, Rivera recalls art objects worth thousands of dollars and others going for a few cents when they are one and the same; the only thing different being the signature. Let us see:

With respect to popular art, intellectuals forget its makers and are not aware, not even when they do technical work in ethnography, that among the makers of those mass productions there are personalities of an impressive distinctive nature who devise and often impose their style. Indeed there are great artists and great masters involved in that marvelous production, who at times pass on to their children and grandchildren their knowledge and genius.

Such is the case of don Tito Reyes and his wife, who understood, in that hovel in *Metepec,* where they lived out of touch with the rest of the world, that color can have great life and potency to animate form when it is not applied initially. That is why don Tito and his wife painted their fired clay sculptures the whitest of whites, on top of which their genius traced marvelous striations of pure color, allowing the purity of those components of light to exist above the form for maximum expression. This gave form an infinitely greater reality than any local tone.

This same discovery in Europe involved the effort of some painters like Picasso, but the work of don Tito has never sold for 20,000 dollars, nor have the critics filled any library with books recommending it. The works of the old man from *Metepec* were available in markets from eighty cents to two pesos per piece, and if they reached the city, they ended up as Mexican curios greatly horrifying our aesthetes.

It would have been another matter if they had been for sale at Chez Rosenberg in Paris or New York, or even if it had taken place 'chez nous' for local collectors of painting on pyroxiline.

All products of popular art are intrinsically the same as the 20,000 prints of José Guadalupe Posada, the masterful works of Velasco, painter of the space of eternity and the retablos of Frida Khalo. All of it is Mexico and forms part of the same exaltation. The only difference among these items isn't due to the object itself but to its producers: it is a difference of class.

Don Tito Reyes, for example, produced for the people and was of the people. He didn't have, or seldom had, intermediaries.

Fortunately for him, those who had his items in their stores were sufficiently stupid to not know they were selling marvelous works of art for a few pennies; they don't know it now when they buy and resell the stupendous white china with line drawings of an extraordinary anonymous female painter, so extraordinary that Picasso painted her in order to 'universalize' her at peace congresses... but at what a different price! Only because Picasso has a known value with the *Chambre Syndicale des Marchands de tableaux et d'objets d'art* whose backers edit in Paris the magazine

Association International des Critiques d'art for their own syndical ends. As we say here, he who serves the church, and lives in the church, is fed by the church.

Rivera can look deeper into popular art and find strange forms of communication, roots, lost links, bits of shipwrecks, and ships without compass. This man could put the people to his ear as if they were a shell and then listen to the waves of the past, voices many of which only he could decipher. He'd stick his hand down the nearest feminine neck and pull out a gold necklace; he'd put the piece on the floor and, with his naked eye alone, examine the piece. He would rush home, filled with ancient treasures and, finding an object that belonged to the night, place it next to the jewel, beginning to smile slowly because, according to him, he had found between them a connection between yesterday and today, a hanging bridge over which, like the great bellied gentleman he was, he could wander and sway up and down as he wished. (During the Colony, he would have been taken for an abbot or a friar.) We mean to say that Diego Rivera showed us his investigative powers, bringing up things that philosophers will have to figure out on their own. We have him here in the flesh, extolling the anonymous artists of Mexico and making quick but definite incursions into the field of psychological science. Seldom have we wandered in fields as interesting as this one where, in spite of the effort to place popular art scientifically where it belongs, it seems as if there remains a hidden, mysterious road through huge trees that, as in those paths in the jungle, leads us to the interior of lost cities. Listen:

What is called in Mexico "popular art," in a way that barely hides its pejorative connotation, is really the survival of a plastic pre-Hispanic tradition often weakened and, in other cases, spoiled through contact with the invaders from the exterior, but live nonetheless. This survival manifests itself often enough in a way that is simply amazing, as much due to the aesthetic quality of its products as for its relation to what is pre-Hispanic. Extraordinary as it is, it also confirms what we have been saying: the most valuable popular art is precisely that which is most directly related to the past. Besides, these works are made by artists who know absolutely nothing of that past and who exercise their plastic capacities on occasion, working the rest of the year in unrelated labors. Such is the case with the cardboard toys we call Judases, being the most disinterested, most pure, and intense expression of present-day Mexican sculpture. Professionals work so far away from ancient Mexican sculpture that I feel obligated to mention it as a fact: these Judases are the best in the world if by that we mean something that reaches beyond itself, in spite of the fact that most of these items are made by people who sculpt only in the days prior to the Saturday after Holy Week.

In *Metepec*, a number of assemblages done in clay and painted in marvelous colors, show characters dancing, playing instruments or listening to music, playing games, getting married, listening to speeches or sermons, celebrating banquets, playing the lottery or gambling, etc. These groups are mounted on disks of clay exactly in the same relationship and using the same techniques as the Colima and Nayarit assemblages featuring dances and other aspects of life in their day. According to specialists, those items go back at least 2,400 years.

This is proof that popular art is no mere reminiscence; don Tito Reyes' grandchildren, producing these extraordinary things, know nothing of the past and have never seen what their forebears made. As a talented critic, eventually spoiled by fascism, said, "In art what is not traditional is pastiche." If, in the case of the contemporary artisans of *Metepec*, there has been no direct learning from ancient masters, we can surmise that tradition has evidently not been continued by any contemporary influence but through that tremendous and obscure phenomenon we know as the subconscious; in reality the work of memory because the cells that form our cortical structure and its glandular extensions, nerves, flesh, and bone, are the same that put together, in the depths of time and in the heart of the waters of the ocean, the protoplasm we live by.

If a child's drawings are a graphic show of the development of a being from past to present, it would be dumb to suppose we can't recall our own life. The opposite is the true tradition. Plato, theorizing on reminiscence, said that 'to learn is to remember'. He verifies our thought, not as an idealist position but dialectically, for the base of our life is cellular activity. So, now we can say, with absolute certainty, that a work of art, and, most specifically, one that comes from the purity of the people, reflects the memory of the species, plus the need for that aesthetic excitation required for our glandular functions and necessary secretions, including the irresistible impulse to create that confirms our own vital potency, receiving from the public what our work is worth, and understanding that the aesthetic emotion is as needed by man as much as his digestive functions.

4

THE BUSINESS OF PRE-HISPANIC ART

On the12th of May, 1950, I had an appointment with Rivera to begin a series of conversations about pre-Hispanic art, beginning with a visit to the galleries where he keeps his fabulous collection. That afternoon, a newspaper scandalized its readers with this news item spread across eight columns: "Diego Rivera Accused of Possessing Stolen Jewels." I got to his place with the paper in my hand, and he began, saying:

One day, as I was painting the *Tenochtitlan* mural at the National Palace, an individual came near me to offer me a few pieces I still conserve of *Jaina* Mayan pottery that he carried in a basket. There were three clay pieces, the most important representing a chief at the moment of receiving prisoners while a warrior looks at him leaning on his shield. The rest of the lot was insignificant, whistles, small items. The whole was worth less than 1,000 pesos. I must tell you that the commerce in ancient art is not illegal. Private collections are permitted as long as this is done within the country. I asked the stranger where he had obtained the pieces and he told me he had bought them but, needing money, was selling them. Subsequently, when doctor Rubín de la Borbolla organized an exposition of pre-Hispanic art in the National Museum, he picked the most interesting pieces from my collection and showed them there, as an indefinite loan on my part.

My intention in buying and collecting the marvelous works of our major art tradition is to keep the same bandits who are accusing me of owning stolen jewels from making a living selling them in the US Each piece in my collection, from the most important to the most insignificant, has been donated to the nation, just as this building I have built here in the Pedregal of San Angel. These gifts, unique in our environment, are covered under the trusteeships of the National College, of which I am a founding member, the National Institute of Bellas Artes, the History and Ethnography Institute, the Regent of Mexico City, and the National Autonomous University of Mexico. My collection then, as the church faithful would say, is 'sanctified' in order to avoid the swipe of the traffickers in art, who are more dangerous than drug dealers.

The fact is that that news item is typical. It's a well-calculated attempt to blackmail a collector, and this has no other object than to confuse collectors, intimidating them and threatening them so that this can facilitate the illegal traffic that could then export works of art freely, a thing presently forbidden.

This illegal trafficking is hard to control due to the technical skills of contrabandists functioning all along our borders; above all because the United States is interested in having our works of art in the hands of their institutes, enriching their culture at the expense of ours. That's all it is. Besides, those who slander an artist, who has dedicated his life to Mexico by writing such news items, are committing a filthy thing, an unqualified rottenness.

When did you begin to collect ancient objects?

When I got to Mexico City, I was six years old. My first two deep emotions were the way grocery stores were painted and the National Museum. Posada had already enchanted me in Guanajuato. Within a few weeks, the museum prevailed over everything else. I was passionate about pre-Hispanic sculpture, and with the few pennies they could give me at home, for we had fallen into penury, I'd go to the Salvador market (today called Lagunilla) and buy small pieces within the reach of my pockets. My father never asked for any favors so when we got here, the only job he could find here was with Public Works, which paid a miserable wage.

Wandering through the stalls on Sunday after Sunday, I got to know by sight don Alfredo Chavero, a circumspect and elegant old man, wearing glasses, but quite myopic, and don Felix Parra, a friendly gentleman with a white beard sticking out. One Sunday, accompanied by my father, he told me their names, adding: "Don Alfredo is an eminent man, a historian and archeologist; Mister Parra is the one who did the portrait of Fray Bartolomé de las Casas. Remember? You talked about him after you visited the galleries of the San Carlos Academy."

I still have in my possession some of the pieces I bought at that time. By the way, one of them was a jade piece of a monkey I bought for one peso. It took me two Sundays to get the money while they kept it for me. When my father's situation got better, my allowance on Sundays went up to three pesos. Unfortunately, many of those pieces I found then were lost in my parents' house during the troubled years, when I was out of the country.

Today, bandits dealing in such articles, were they to fall into their paws and beaks, would make a considerable amount of money. But in those days it wasn't strange to find archeological pieces as door stops, or serving to hold down a clothesline the minute you went out to a nearby town. Without going too far back, since such things took place more than fifty years ago, don Luis Castillo Ledón, already the director of the National Museum, found a huge, marvelous, jade sculpture one Sunday in a shop selling fresh water at the entrance of a greenhouse in *Coyoacan*. He had a lot of trouble getting it since it served a support. For the old lady to part with it, he had to bring her a large rock and pay her five honest-to-God pesos out of his own pocket; a painful sacrifice since he donated the piece to the Museum.

The origins of my collection were likewise. Upon returning to Mexico, the first piece that I acquired was the marvelous jadeite mask of the kind called *Olmec*, a work which Carlos Mérida had found in *Olinalá*. Working with me in the amphitheatre of the Preparatory National School, he was obliged to sell it to me since what our Maecenas paid us was so miserable that if someone got sick in our house, there was no money for medicines. Due to an illness of his wife, he had to sell the mask to me, excusing himself for asking quite a bit, since he adored it. With a sorrowful face he asked for seventy-five pesos! A trafficker today wouldn't let it go for less than a thousand dollars; in New York he might get two-thousand for it. But that was the situation in those days, what you asked for and what you spent for pieces much superior to those gangsters will kill for.

The phenomenon of the exploitation and stealing of preclassic art on a grand scale is done in this form: In the first stage of an imperialist action, politicians, diplomats, and after that, the army and the marines, jump to the attack in case the country about to be devoured tries to resist.

If there are marines and boot soldiers, the military forces are joined by the camp followers who trek behind every conquering army. Pillage is the rule. Bankers get hold of the financial machinery, the industrialists grab the raw materials, the thieves and merchants assault the markets of the victim nation. There are also bandits expert in the sciences and the arts who pilfer the culture of that country, and thieves who steal what they ignore, admirals who order the bombardment of the Acropolis, and generals who lead armies of outlaws to sack Peking's imperial palace on the pretext of attacking the 'boxers' who were really nothing but exalted patriots, much less brutal than those who form the Ku Klux Klan.

As a result of all this, the imperialist metropolises receive the artworks of the conquered country as booty. There follow two stages in order to make capital out of them. First they pretend to ignore them so that the professional speculators can divide the goods. The second stage is diffusion; the merchants and the museums make timely expositions, and the sharp critics discover the high aesthetic quality of the stolen and reconsidered objects, writing articles and books about them. Simultaneously, from the time the artists of the imperialist metropolis discover those objects in the galleries of dealers, they discuss them, admire them, grope them, and end up imitating them. This imitation is the slap on the back of the aesthetic value of the booty. At that moment, the private collectors are ready to acquire the stolen fruit and the clever and discreet imitations that they at first disdain but end up paying quite a bit for.

This is what took place with the art of the Orient. Its influence began with Monet and was exalted by Van Gogh and Gauguin, passing from them to Picasso and his contemporaries. The modest Japanese and Chinese prints followed the normal course of events until the local production went up in value while still connected to the imported objects. Toulouse-Lautrec, without understanding them, painted true euro-Japanese masterpieces on boards sold on makeshift holiday stands. He achieved decent returns forty years after his death when they sold for millions of francs, dozens of thousands of dollars. The same happened with the brilliant works of Van Gogh and with the talented and nostalgic paintings of Gauguin which, presented on the sidewalks and small stores of Montmartre, nobody wanted for one or two hundred francs, today considered real bargains when you can find them for 20,000 dollars; the equivalent of several million francs.

Japan, China, India, Siam, Indochina, Bali, and all the marvelous Pacific Islands suffered from armed military pillage, as did all of Africa. In Africa, it was done in such a brutal form that the functionaries returned to Paris, Brussels, and Berlin loaded with the result of their exploitation and carnage. The native art was so extraordinary, so intense, so vigorous, and therefore so distant from the pomades, perfumes, and Parisian fashions, that it rolled down to the flea markets and filled the showcases of the Trocadero ethnographic museum. It had been gathered by the scientific missions accompanying the infantry killers in Africa without being 'discovered' aesthetically by anyone except for the smartest painters and sculptors, the seasoned and malicious men of the 'extreme left.' Thus, a very long time before black African sculpture was sold for millions of dollars, it showed up copied with genius and without shame beneath the veils of Cezannism in the Ladies of Avignon by today's omnipotent and omnipresent Picasso, whose genius was utilized by merchants all the way to the Communist Party, after passing through duchesses, queens of kotex and sugar, and all manner of wealthy Latin Americans.

For a long time, the painters and sculptors with the greatest plastic sensitivity have looked to America. Many of Picasso's extraordinary inventions had already been made in Peru and *Tlatilco* thousands of years ago, others from *Tenochtitlán* date back five thousand years. But Picasso is a she-wolf. His gospel is that axiom of some critical poet: "In art, plagiarism is perfectly legal and valued as long as it is followed by assassination." This makes perfect sense to Pablo Picasso in connection with hundreds of innocent painters who went to him seeking money and were totally despoiled. But murder is much more difficult when dealing with ancient forms of art; the thieving painter then plays dead or at least dumb while his originals haven't arrived at the world of the great public.

For several years now, the gentlemen of the Syndicate of Dealers in Paintings and Art Objects had taken note of our pre-Hispanic art and had quietly begun accumulating their stocks. But there was an obstacle facing them, as was told to me with perfect frankness thirty-five years ago by the then sculptor and dealer, later a millionaire in New York: Mister Brummer. The inconvenience was the fact that there were collectors of ancient Mexican art in Mexico, which meant that there was in existence a previous price level and a certain awareness of values out of the control of organized speculators. There were also two serious obstacles: the enormous abundance of certain objects of high aesthetic quality (and by that token difficult to assign a large value to them), plus the incredible ability of Mexicans faking ancient works of art. This puts a lot of stress and difficulty in front of merchants wanting to speculate without the help of Mexican experts. The most conspicuous foreign professionals have suffered tremendous and comic failures in the field of authenticity (difficult to say whose loss this was), for they lacked a profound and complete knowledge of the matter; they lack the subtle sensitivity that can differentiate between an original and a fake.

Mister Brummer, who had begun to go into the pre-colonial Mexican art business full blast, had to abandon it in disgust. He sold the pieces he had managed to collect, since he was duped into buying high-priced fakes. This seriously shook his professional reputation and he died soon after; such a terrible failure was probably connected with his death.

This situation, made worse by the increasing interest in ancient and contemporary Mexican art, has created events ranging from the Chaplin-like comic to tragic trials in court, features in police gazettes, including premeditated murder, treachery, and gain.

When it comes to Mexico, the looting of ancient art is not anything new, but its character has changed. We are far away from the time when the traveling French photographer Claude Joseph Desiré Charnay (author of the book *Le Mexique, Souvenirs et Impressions),* turned archeologist so as to be allowed to photograph the bas-reliefs in a Mayan building, dynamited one of its walls. We no longer live in those times when English men of science, sent here with great generosity by Lord Kingsburg, with the notion that, by studying the Mayas, they could prove they were the lost tribe of Israel. They found a notarized inventory at a hacienda in *Chichén Itzá* listing, among other valuables, "many tons of carved stone..." referring to the master works of the most extraordinary sculpted and painted archeology in the world which the darling *Yucatec* landowners felt obliged to let the Englishman and his employees (famous men of science and letters) take away to British museums and private collections. They also took white cement samples ripped off painted masterpieces from *Teotihuacán,* inspiring the "invention" of Portland cement around that time in the United Kingdom, something that earned them billions of pounds.

This was probably the most important looting of our culture, economically speaking.

We are past the times when the Great Necklace of the Red eagle, given to don Porfirio Diaz by the Kaiser, resulted in having the learned Dr. Eduard Seler cart away to Germany such a great quantity of large boxes full of marvelous monoliths, that even during the beginning of WWI nineteen cases filled with such treasures were left behind in Brussels. Fortunately, we heard about it in France. Luis Quintanilla, then Mexican minister in Paris, Francisco Orozco Muñoz and I, managed to have the boxes held in liberated Brussels through the Belgian Minister, so they never got to the museum in Berlin, but I have to tell you that they didn't get in the Brussels' museum either. They never got back to Mexico. I can assure you that this was a fruitless diplomatic adventure in a pre-continental style for an important diplomat from our country.

The time is also long gone when a sinister Mr. Thompson purchased the *Chichen Itza* hacienda in order to sack jade and other precious objects in gold and fine stones, besides carved stones, with an up-to-date steam dredger in the very place where our dazzling, ancient forefathers had thrown them in propitiatory sacrifices. This Thompson covered up his act with a consular investiture from his country. It was necessary for the socialist revolutionary movement of the martyr Carrillo Puerto and his temporary position as the governor of Yucatan to kick out the insolent mechanized robber.

Things have changed a bit, my dear Cardona, but our own National Museum continued to have a completely ridiculous budget for acquisitions. This condition continued for ethnography, archeology, anthropology and Mexican history until the advent of Alfonso Caso, who managed to better somewhat the shameful penury of the museum. Imagine! All he had to purchase key objects for the nation that might have cost several thousand pesos, was the formidable sum of one hundred and twenty-five pesos annually.

It was still that way when my friend Luis Castillo Ledón, the biographer of Hidalgo, took over the reigns of the museum. Because of that, it isn't strange that while the institute saw marvel after marvel offered to it come and go without being able to purchase them, the museum of the University of Tulane was enriching its collection. This was told to me by my friend, Frans Blom. When he became director, it had, according to him, four showcases for our objects, including those from Central America, which are as much ours as our own.

With the economic and protective collaboration of my friend, the truly illustrious Madame Matilde Gray, and other persons of good taste, who had a selfless interest in the culture of their country, the museum in Tulane had three hundred showcases with pre-Hispanic objects, while ours had half a dozen.

As I have told you, my dear friend, it has been more than thirty years since the antiquarian Brummer was interested in Mexican ancient art and was testing the possibilities of making some purchases. He'd repeat to me with each conversation: "The trouble is that, as I have heard, there are several collectors of that kind of art in Mexico." He'd say this because dealers in art objects hate the fact that when they estimate the worth of an art that hasn't yet been 'valued' by the market, there are persons possessing a considerable quantity of the very same objects they wish to speculate with.

It's one of two things: either the original collectors, when they get wind of the rise in prices, hurry to offer their pieces in the large markets, ruining the purchasing power of private collectors, or these compete with the dealers to the point of invalidating any speculation.

Besides, the prestige and authority of the original experts, as well as those experts and critics in their pocket, present a real danger to the assessment of the kind of values that the professional dealers seek. In spite of this inconvenience, Brummer had buyers in Mexico starting twenty years ago. They managed to take away, for him exclusively, masterpieces of fundamental importance to Mexico, like a marvelous woman giving birth. This sculpture, unique in the world, after being Brummer's, ended up in the incredibly distinguished hands of the collector of modern art and excellent critic, Mr. Walter Arensberg of Los Angeles, who owns a magnificent collection of pre-Hispanic Mexican art.

It is the same with the great dramatic actor Charles Laughton, who owns a collection of the highest quality, above all, pieces from western Mexico.

It is interesting to note that while our urban authorities hurl themselves against the poor 'idol' makers in the provinces, and while some governments, like those of the states of Colima, Nayarit and Jalisco decide to set up local museums, shady persons (some of them connected to public administrations and therefore big buddies of governors and customs officials) find the way to take enough objects out of the country to form collections involving prestigious quantities of dollars.

No matter how valuable they are from an artistic point of view, collections such as those of Arensberg and Laughton are several degrees less important than the collection of the millionaire senator Robert Woods Bliss. Forming part of his collection, besides numerous stones, precious jades, tempting obsidian items, bright gold, and crystallized rocks, it has nothing less than an authentic masterwork of all time, a *Teotihuacán* fresco, to be seen at the National Gallery in Washington D. C.

Our functionaries in the fields of archeology, ethnography, and history, have made diplomatic gestures to soften the heart of senator Bliss and persuade him to return to Mexico what was an integral part of a national monument since the fresco was attached to the wall of one of the buildings discovered not so long ago in *Teotihuacán.* But in spite of the fact that the senator has been offered a full reimbursement for what he might have paid for it, his patriotism has not been shaken and he has preferred to place the fresco (which he acquired from the hands of traffickers) as a loan to the National Gallery, instead of returning it to the *Teotihuacán* building, where a gaping hole continues to exist among other admirable frescoes.

But how were they able to get it out of there and sell it in the United States?

It's a long story, but an extremely interesting one. Look here: several years ago, digging a ditch to add a kitchen to a hut, a painted wall was discovered near the *Teotihuacán* archeological zone. The hut had been built on top of a hillock, which, like hundreds of others in the Valley, contained extraordinary ancient monuments.

Those who found the fresco discovered next to it a site of small admirable clay figures. And I, wandering around one day looking for whatever, was offered them for sale by the workers who took a liking to me. They showed me the section of the wall containing the painting, of which only some twenty-five centimeters were visible.

I mentioned the interest I had to an archeologist friend of mine, and talked to another one who was higher up in the official hierarchy, but he didn't consider the matter very important.

"There must be so much there!" he exclaimed. "It's an impossibility to explore it all! I don't have enough people and hardly any money. If an extraordinary administration were to give me five million pesos, I could organize a general search but not an exploration. I have to first of all get together the necessary personnel."

I didn't think about the matter any longer until the antiquarian Guillermo Echaniz asked me several times to go by his house to look at a *Teotihuacán* fresco that he had. The piece, it must be said, had been torn off the wall with great care. It was encased in a rough wooden box, but it was well anchored. My friend, the archeologist Porfirio Aguirre, had made a paper copy of it. Echaniz was in a bad mood, desperate because he had found no buyer for the work, which naturally required a long and difficult process of restoration and placement in an adequate case. When I pointed out to Echaniz the difficulty of the situation, for it was obvious that the painting belonged to the country, even though it hadn't been catalogued by official science (that most prudent of sciences, slow, wearing glasses), he told me: "Give me what it has cost me to bring it up to this stage, since it most likely would have been torn to bits by those who found it..." And I thought, "Why hasn't he notified the Institute? After all is said, he is an honest businessman."

Echaniz added, "Give me eight hundred pesos. You can decide whether to keep it or turn it in." I would have loved to give him his eight-hundred pesos and with the evidence on hand, I would have convinced my friends to continue exploring that location, but I didn't have the eight-hundred pesos, and was about to leave the country in a few hours.

When I returned home, I heard that the piece was still in Echaniz's warehouse. My friend Caso, chief of the Institute, had seen the copy made by Aguirre but had thought it was a joke. There was talk that the fresco was a falsification, and no one from the official world went to look at the original.

I insisted, to the point of impertinence, that the piece be kept in its original place. I was perhaps even rude, but I got nowhere. I am being precise when I say that I don't know why that was.

Much later, in 1940, I went to Los Angeles, California, and while visiting the gallery of my friend Stendhal, dealer in paintings and other art objects, I found the fresco in the restoration shop next to his gallery, where they also manufactured wonderful chocolates. A year later, I returned to Mexico and mentioned it to Caso, insisting on its importance and giving him the exact address where the fresco was to be found. But even while its existence was now acknowledged, its authenticity and the quality of the copy were still a matter of discussion.

I got nowhere. Several years had to go by until—finally—official archeology agreed to go to the place where the masterpiece had been found and, beside the empty hole the fresco had occupied, discovered marvels there. I insisted we should check another wall sticking up nearby as a temptation to profane and not archeological eyes. We found there another superb fresco that came to light precisely when an exposition of art from the western part of Mexico was being held in Bellas Artes.

In that exhibition, one of my own 'sets' of ball players was displayed. But friends of mine, archeologists from the School of Law, didn't see any ball players; they saw warriors or gods and smiled with compassion when I'd point to the batter with his helmet and his shield, the catcher with his *chacuallí* (which I myself used as a kid in the San Camilo gym), and the leader who threw the ball that started the game. They smiled at me and said, or thought "That's Diego!..." But, lo and behold! The painted wall in *Teotihuacán* came to life and there wasn't one but several batters hitting the ball. Nevertheless, archeologists, who are most serious, kept repeating. "Nothing in the chronicles of the conquest points to any other game but the one that was played using the waist, and no codex shows players using their hands or a bat." They forgot that the Colima figures of players, as was proved by objects found subsequently during scientific excavations, were contemporary with the *Teotihuacán* wall showing ball players, batters, catchers, and pitchers.

Would it be too much to ask the wise to recognize the meridian fact that in those times when the *Teotihuacán* and Occidental cultures coincided with how they functioned, that no monks or laymen writing chronicles had yet arrived, but that not even *Tenochtitlán* had yet been founded by the Aztecs?

They also fail to realize that there are diverse ways and styles to play ball games but, anyway, when Dr. Caso wanted to correct his error, the fresco was already in the United States, in the merchant hands of Stendhal, who passed it to the soft and famous claws of the all-powerful Senator Bliss, occupying a prominent place in his collection. That's when all manner of great means were employed to get it back: persuasion, diplomacy, cash propositions, smiles, gifts, gold-plated placards in which the illustrious donor would be acknowledged, as well as the friendly pressure of my friend, the excellent and learned Chester Dale, the biggest and best collector of French painting of the XVII to the XXth centuries.

Everything failed. Nothing was able to touch the Yankee patriotism, perfectly legitimate, of Senator Bliss. The Mexican monument remained mutilated and the fresco proudly exhibited by its new owner in the National Gallery in Washington, DC. But after all, one can also find, on the other side, on indefinite loan, many other Mexican items, among them, the territories of California, Texas, Colorado, and New Mexico, besides a few more insignificancies.

In what ways do the traffickers of high rank manage to carry out their operations dealing with the ancient art of Mexico?

This traffic involves three intangibles, which are: first, those covered by what we could call scientific immunity; second, those covered by social immunity; and, third, those covered by diplomatic immunity. The last is the most delicate and insoluble of the three.

Scientific immunity involves the heads or famous members of important institutions coming to Mexico on missions of their own. Our country spends more money on soccer or polo equipment than in explorations that would help create a historical consciousness of the homeland and make folk proud of their past, without which the country could never act in a reasonable way in the present, and much less build bases for its future. Because of this it is not possible to refuse; we must find the way to collaborate and seek the help of foreign scientific institutions and have them come and realize what is indispensable, since our own institutes lack the means to do it. In consequence of which, foreign missions can't be treated as if by a police regime. We tolerate the fact that, behind the apparent strict compliance with the law and any contracts, objects that obviously should remain with us depart with those missions to their country of origin. And it isn't possible to complain. It is preferable to argue that knowledge of our archeology is helpful and admired in distant museums.

Those with social immunity include people from the lowest to the highest ranks of the artistic, literary and political world. It includes the friendship of functionaries that, due to that friendship, makes it difficult to react in cases of illegal exports. I personally know artists of value who, from time to time get tired of their small jade objects and other such items, having acquired valuable collections, so when they travel abroad, carry them to sell there. Small objects are easily transported in a coat pocket or a pair of pants, and once they are beyond our borders or catch a plane, they do it as if it is their right to do it. There are gold detectors but none for jade or rock crystals. The object can also hang from the neck of a beautiful lady and, traveling in that marvelous place, arrive safely in New York or any other place on earth.

Sometimes, the collector artist is so fond of one of his pieces that he doesn't want to leave it behind in Mexico so he takes it with him to continue to enjoy it on his journey. At least, that's what he says.

I recall how a friend of mine, some thirty years ago, had a soapbox full of jade pieces. When an eminent and powerful American lady arrived here in her private Pullman, he begged an American friend of his to have the lady take it in her Pullman. It was done and the owner of the soapbox and the box, were transported to New York. Months or years later, those traveling objects appeared reproduced in monograms in art magazines that publish things owned by the big millionaire collectors in the States.

As far as scientific immunity goes, I won't make reference to embassy secretaries with low pay but long poker or canasta sessions, creating circumstances that increase the volume, density and variety of diplomatic luggage, but I will recall my good, fine, and distinguished friend, Count K, minister in Mexico from his majesty the king of the Belgians. The Count became passionate about Mexican art and archeology and, with the help of a few assessors at his service, some of them antiquarians, he made numerous acquisitions, some of them magnificent and others of dubious authenticity but of obvious beauty. He never hid his purchases from functionaries of the Department of Archeology, whom he would invite to see his important acquisitions, to ask if an object was unique or had equivalents in the official collections.

But war came and the diplomat left. No one was surprised when he took those works of art with him. Surely, due to the hazards of armed conflict, many of the most important pieces he had collected ended up in the market for antiquities in New York.

Without splitting too many hairs, let us recall the eminent archeologist Elizabeth Kelly, from the University of California. She made very valuable explorations in the west of the country and provided new and extremely valuable data about the archeology of the region, bringing to the capital an enormous quantity of material. Those interested in these matters speak of the number of tons that was involved. Half of it remained in Mexico, the other half went to the 'other side,' with the investigator. She paid the expenses for all the work thanks to a scientific institution in her country, as the contractual stipulations read. Consequently, the matter was one hundred percent legal. But wouldn't it have been a thousand times preferable to have funded the explorations with Mexican money? That way we wouldn't have lost half of what belonged to us. The entire exploration would have cost less than a trip by a sports delegation. And we don't mean to say we shouldn't have such delegations going to foreign places, but that we should remember that scientific work benefits the nation. The case of the eminent female archeologist is not unique. One could make long lists of similar cases. All such explorations that pay the Maecenas aesthetically for the expenses incurred; that is why foreign collections grow at the expense of the national ones.

The location of the brick-making factories of San Luis *Tlatilco* constitute, as once explained by the painter Miguel Covarrubias, "the richest, most cosmopolitan, and surely the most important center of the pre-classic cultures of the Valley of Mexico." In spite of that, the most extensive and scientific explorations have only been made in the last few years, between 1947 and 1949, under the auspices of the Viking Fund, which shared the management of the work with a group of enthusiastic young Mexican archeologists.

Tlatilco, which in *Nahuatl* means a place 'where there are hidden things,' became the richest and the most surprising of all the pantheons in Mexico; fundamental to establish the ancient and fabulous chronology of pre-Hispanic art in the central region.

We wanted to close this chapter with a dissertation by Rivera on the artistic production of that zone. This is what he said:

Tlatilco's clayey soil, perfect for the manufacture of bricks, guards in its strata items from the most remote of our cultures to the most modern archaic period, going back 2,500 years; say, less than half the amount of what was preserved under the lava of the Pedregal de San Angel.

Against the archeological opinion of the past and present, using the means and machines that measure molecular cohesion with the precision that an electrocardiogram traces its curves, the lava at Pedregal has been dated to be 7,000 years old, a date which, with no more instruments than his brain, my teacher Ezequiel Odoñez had proposed. This admirable geologist gave the British Empire the oil of Mesopotamia and was named a lord, but 99 percent of our population knows nothing of the great man.

In *Tlatilco* our most ancient cultures were stratified. This discovery wasn't made by any professional from the archeological world, not even anyone with some education but by the brick makers whose work is destined to make horrendous houses in today's capital. They do commerce with the sacred clay of our land while it has been impossible to declare the place an archeological zone. When I tried as a busybody, not being an archeologist or an ethnographer, but with the insolence that authorizes me due to this crazy love I have for my country, to urge my friend Dr. Alfonso Caso to declare that venerable place an archeological zone, he replied, "That's fine, Diego; the pieces from *Tlatilco* charm me as much as they do you, but… what is *Tlatilco*? To this day I don't understand his question. Today, those working under Dr. Daniel R. de la Borboll, director of the National Museum of Anthropology, know, as we all do, what *Tlatilco* is. It is an immensely important living cemetery, a veritable open book about our past. But it is urgent to close the brick factories that are destroying that precious ground. Don't let anyone argue, as some have, that 500 workers would be left without a job because there is plenty of clay elsewhere in the state. A stroke of the pen from above, could provide twenty times more clay to make all the bricks wanted without harming anyone instead of continuing to destroy the nation's past. The miniscule interests of the honorable owners of the brick ovens could be honored by compensating them for their loss. The interests of the nation, with its 30 million inhabitants, come first, and not 500 *Tlatilco* workers, it being ironic that these belong to the social class that saw two million killed during our Mexican Revolution.

But these indisputable and irrefutable arguments, for anyone who is not a unique and shameless idiot, are not the only ones. There is the most important reason of all: that of beauty.

The different types of sculpture found in *Tlatilco* are, without doubt, the most original, refined, praised, and subtle of ancient Mexican sculpture. Sure, Mayan work at its best rose to an insuperable delicacy and elegance, but *Tlatilco's* art, through its evolution in time, doesn't lag behind, reaching levels in terms of character and imagination beyond that of the Mayas. For example, the creation of the bicephalous woman, presented at times as ultra-sensible beings. Sapho wouldn't have asked for anything better in presenting her preference for the same great grace, maximum beauty, and extreme intelligence, that Plato referred to as the love that is purely feminine. It could be said that Sapho—poetry itself—should have been the model for the first of those double-headed representations.

This bicephalous aspect can be interpreted in two ways: as the plastification of a rhythmic movement in dance, or as a portrait of a teratological case definitely elevated to a religious category. These hypotheses disappear when we observe different kinds of double-headed women. Within the same style we find the delicate, ultra-sensible and ultra-aristocratic. We also find them as dancers with enormous hips and as what we might call realistic portraits, where the individual character and the anatomic proportions are treated with definite aim at style, with no alterations. But we also encounter them in the field of humor, marvelous portraits of super fat hams, with the biting expression of an implacable critical sense.

This diversity proves the hypothesis that inter-feminine love is much truer than any other, because of the acute and totally specific beauty adequate to its representation (one without equal in any other part of the world). We have there groups of women in the most obvious of love dialogues, unequivocal not only because of the gestures, but due to the inevitable emotion emanating from these small masterpieces.

As if this were not enough, in the marvelous and extraordinary art of *Tlatilco,* woman dominates as the central theme. When a male appears, if it isn't when a mother carries him in her arms, the male personage is invariably criticized, sometimes with a caustic, disdainful ferocity.

The clay technique in the culture of *Tlatilco* is so subtle that, for example, the manner in which the statues are individualized results in portraits of an amazing kind. This is obtained by applying an extremely delicate clay mask over the generalized head, gaining intensity and inspiration from tiny inflections of form. The individualization is completed with the characteristics of the headdresses since the sculptures of *Tlatilco* present an enormous variety of adornments. Given these conditions, one would be tempted to say that the main part of the figurines have no equal in the world. They were modeled by female artists. What has survived today of the extraordinary art of the peoples of Mexico, frequently presents cases of feminine potters of insuperable quality.

As it may well be, and completely on the margin of aesthetic fantasy, of scientific or political hypothesis, or all that combined, is the fact that *Tlatilco's* art, due to its plastic value containing profound human emotions, is without doubt one of the highest, strongest, and most original expressions of human art.

5

CRITICS AND CRITIQUES

In this chapter, Rivera uses in his exposition the Marxist dialectic to focus on the aspects of the theme as follows:

When talking of art criticism, it is necessary first of all to clarify its nature and its functions. Works of art appear to almost coincide with the first vestiges of human culture that prove the presence of man in time. But its quality, or the potential to produce the phenomenon we call aesthetic emotion can't be considered as primitive in terms of time, but only in relation to the means of work employed, those tools that determine the specific character of the technique because the capacity to produce aesthetic emotion, namely beauty, is found in the most ancient works of art that we know, possessing an intensity no lesser but greater than what humanity has produced subsequently.

Those group paintings of mammoths, bison, horses, deer, bulls, buffaloes, giraffes, elks and tigers hunting, feeding, or hurriedly fleeing and jumping in landscapes of an extraordinary veracity formed by the very accidents of the rocks on which they are painted, have really never been equaled or bettered, as we mentioned when discussing the art found in caverns. All this obligates us to find the real cause of the phenomenon.

In order to do it, we have to analyze the conditions of life within which such works were produced, finding that which characterizes that epoch is the absence of classes. The men who lived then were free, understanding that by freedom we mean no oppression, control or exploitation by individuals, groups, castes, or classes in power. This lets us arrive at the conclusion that, on one side, the greater the direct contact of the maker of this art with the organic life of matter, and the greater his liberty, the capacity to produce an aesthetic emotion is in direct relation with the conditions mentioned. And we are obliged to deduce that the more that human society develops through time, those in power largely attempt to control and direct the works of art, both form and content, in a way that is favorable to their own interests. Thus, after the marvelous cave paintings and stupendous sculptures contemporary with them, all within a frame that was absolutely free, as if it wasn't the complying with vital functions, there begins that "cosmic terror" that master Spengler talked about: fear of hunger and pain begin, and above all, fear of death, which terrorizes humans in proportion to their ignorance of it. If they understood the vital role of death, the phenomenon of transformation that it is, they wouldn't tremble before that act of love, the most profound of all.

With all the terrors that death brought on, the most astute individuals among the first human groups formed the basis for a system of myths which, in a practical way, meaning an optimistic fashion, created magic as a way to tame out-of-control forces. From magic, later on, came science which, in its mystical application, (meaning pessimistic and self-destroying) produced religion, the attempt to detain the consequences of natural forces by submitting to them, forces personified as beings similar to humans, who could be approached with sacrificial gifts. Those in power got invested, when they could, into the category of magicians, priests, and warriors. It was necessary to remain in power through terror of physical force, a situation that gave birth to theocracy. When a chief could not or didn't think it necessary to be the magician, priest or warrior, he would simulate them, a situation that has prevailed to this day in every place on earth where popular socialist power has not been installed.

By the same token that those in power rely on the collaboration of warriors, magicians, or men of science (today we have atomic magicians), they also need the help of the producers of aesthetic emotion, in other words, of artists, since a work of art, thanks to the pleasure it produces, can alleviate and compensate by some measure for the pain of exploitation. And if it can achieve this through form, it can also do it through content. It can surely be an instrument helping power by the diffusion of religious and secular lies aiding in the exploitation of people. Religion, morality, and law are the means. Or it could be converted into an effective weapon against lying to the people, teaching it to discover, through its contents, the lies power uses to exploit it. This last is realism, and its actual and most complete expression is socialist realism.

Criticism functions doubly as:

A: The analytically scientific examination of the historical situation that has produced the work of art.

B: The deduction, following this analysis, of conclusions that fatally incline to this or that social interest.

In any case, it couldn't be but on the side of those who manage exploitative power, or on the side of the people struggling against it. A neutral position couldn't be sustained because if the criterion of the critic pretends to avoid any political position, he will have done nothing more than to take, beneath the appearance of a third position uninvolved in the social struggle between classes (philosophy, art for art's sake, etc.), a truly hypocritical position. Of course, this attitude favors those in power and distances itself from the interests of the exploited. Besides, it permits the critic and the false artist to sell their aesthetic narcotics and their silence to those "at the top" at the same time that they convey to the exploited the necessary tranquilizer to lessen their pain and eliminate any energy for the struggle.

As we well know, the constant use of tranquilizers takes you to a toxic state so that, even if the people assume power, to continue selling these poisons to them is equivalent to weakening them painfully. That is why it is necessary to denounce these traffickers of toxic music, painting, sculpture and literature, even when socialist power has been achieved.

The bourgeoisie and its providers have been thunderous about protecting liberty when the Soviet government told artists pretending to serve the people what the people wanted and needed. Why? Because it saw the danger that those human groups who haven't yet achieved their own government and true liberty might refuse intoxicating products. This is a tremendous danger for exploiting governments that use aesthetic toxins—moral and religious—to convert its citizens into zombies. Nevertheless, there is no attack against the freedom of composers, poets or painters if they like to produce what is not consumable in a socialist market; all they have to do is move to Paris, New York or Mexico to find their market.

Surely, a socialist people would be pleased with that migration, just as we feel happy when we are cured from hives. For their part, the bourgeoisie would be happy to employ and buy those 'free' products that please them so much.

Because of this, there is nothing more pernicious than those critics who appear to be political, who claim to be on the left, but who, in the exercise of their criticism, bolster products that are aesthetically harmful to popular interests and attack those that are good for people. The art critic in a capitalist society, independently of his knowledge and literary faculties, and independent also from the enthusiasm and sincerity he might show in the carrying out of his work, is nothing more or less than the advertiser of merchandise, and this merchandise might be nutritive for the neuro-glandular apparatus of a people or poisonous for it. In any case, his work is subject to the iron laws of the economy. On the first page of the "Critique of Political Economy" one can read the following:

"Merchandise is that which is useful to the life of man. It doesn't matter whether this need involves the digestive apparatus or the imagination."

A work of art involves both... and how!: The living expenses of artists, the profit for the dealer in art and for the collectors and, fatally, compensation for the hours of labor that a critic might need. Here we must repeat the priests and priestesses of the 33.33 percent, He who serves the church and lives off it, is fed by the church. Here "by the church" is meant art and its artists. The critics are the priests, and the businessmen the merchants at the temple. Oh, but there exist, Cardona, my friend, the *Chambre syndicale des marchants de tableaux et d'objets d'art* and the *Société Internationale des critiques d'art.*

You might ask, What is hidden behind those pompous names? I would answer, Both form an immensely respectable institution. Business involving them is international in nature and the monies involved reach hundreds of millions of dollars; billions of francs given their monetary evaluation.

In that syndical chamber, dealers in paintings and other objects of art come together and reach agreements, naturally, for the defense and protection of their interests. The commerce of aesthetic material is a hugely important aspect of the economies of France and the whole of Europe, representing one of the few possibilities of defense against the depreciation of European monetary value in relation to Yankee currency. For over fifty years the United States have been the best market for paintings from the Old World, principally the French, which has had the best propaganda and administration in place. This has been so since Paris is the largest producer of art in the world, where painting of all kinds and for all tastes is made, providing, with its very important auxiliary, architecture, the proper tone to its style.

The immediate auxiliaries to this business are the art critics, the museum directors, the top employees of all the departments of fine arts in the world, the historians of art, the investigators of aesthetics, the inspectors in charge of controlling the entry and disposal of fine art past frontier customs as well as those in charge of caring for museums and monuments who decide what art objects can or cannot be sold, especially archeological items. They includes all those whose speculations, commercial gains, open or hidden commissions in the buying and selling of beautiful objects, official or private wages, and that whole scale of the graft that is possible within this vast apparatus for those who live and steal in the shadow of art.

We should add the play of the stock market where the ups and downs in the price of art works takes place, affecting not only auctions, but their regular price in galleries. Besides that, we have the end-game of the critics, those who try to take advantage, as well as the apostles of good faith –who exist, though it might seem impossible—functioning consciously or unconsciously, but at all times effectively in the rise and fall of artistic merchandise, acting like salesmen with loudspeakers.

We might add that critics, who are the key in this complicated international speculation resembling a racket, together with the authors of beautiful things, are the victims of the sharpest, most shameless and unpunished international gangsters who go by the pompous name of *marchants des tableaux et des objects d'art*. What these victims manage to charge the bandits they serve is absolutely insignificant compared to what their bosses make. So, given the disproportion between the two, the most exploited victims are the makers of art, followed immediately by critics.

Oh, the critics! They are truly the poorest paid of the broadcasters of the largest speculations. It shouldn't seem strange then, that certain gentlemen and ladies who profess to be critics of art, upon reaching old age, finding themselves at the edge of physical blindness without having accumulated any capital, arrive at the doors of major government bureaucrats and more or less important dealers, to sell favors of political value that translate into wages for some and high financial gain for others, allowing them to raise the price of the merchandise they praise and lower that of criticized work in order to acquire it when worth little and sell it later at high and even very high prices. We already know that the function of criticism, as of everything in life, is dialectical, and that which is valued today is demeaned in twenty years, and vice versa. All of that permits the stock games that bring millions to the gentlemen thieves in galleries and syndicated chambers, dignified brothers of the stock market and of the entire financial capitalist apparatus which crushes the value of the productions of all workers in the world, from the peon and the poorest paid worker to the fat captains of industry, including artists of all kinds.

Among critics, the only ones that escape being victims are those who form the sharpest and most curious sub-species; perhaps we should say super-species: the collectors. The man or woman dedicated to this noble activity without sufficient capital, is lost. On the other hand, those with the means, even with little intelligence or ability, can have a marvelous future. This admirable species is made up of the critic, historian, or investigator who is at the same time a collector, a buyer who in due time turns seller.

The collector-critic, who in Mexico begins to have a few pieces, is nothing new; his antecedents go back probably to a time before the Renaissance. Let's venture a guess and say that his illustrious ancestor could be Petronius. But without second-guessing, we can start with the divine Pietro Aretino, the most shameless Italian poet of the XV and XVI centuries. Do you recall his *sonneti lussoriosi*? What a wonder! Aretino had the nerve to canter his horse at the same pace as that of emperor Charles V during his triumphal entry into Rome, obliging imperial glory to put itself at the service of the literary glory of the most illustrious and genial of the blackmailers, swindlers and procurers at the service of the great of the earth (excepting, naturally, political emperors such as Charles I of Spain and Charles V of Germany, or emperors of art such as the great Titian Vecellio, originally from Pieve di Cadore but Venetian through his genius).

There are extant precious documents listing services from the divine blackmailer to Titian, the portentous master. We must remember, as Guido Caprotti used to say, that "Italian painting during the Renaissance was an enormous industry which Italy produced and exported by the ton to the entire world." And, of course, as with all major industries, competition was tremendous. That is why Titian, the most elegant of masters (since he had the elegance to be in love with his extraordinarily beautiful daughter Lavinia), could or had to write a letter to the divine blackmailer Pietro Aretino referring to one of his disciples of no less talent than himself, perhaps of greater talent (Paris Bordone de Treviso) as follows: "This scoundrel, not content with learning more than I wanted to teach him, has had the insolence not only to paint portraits of professional people, charging them handsomely, but the miserable cur has had the incredible and intolerable nerve to paint the roofs of some palaces of the city, and even more, what is absolutely intolerable, a circular plate and a *panneau* mural in the palace of His Majesty. I hereby order you to take care of him without fault. Don't leave him with a single unbroken bone. You will speak of him in such a way that no one in Venice, not even a stranger passing through, can dare pose for his portrait or make an even more important request than those he has had the nerve to undertake, thinking that his insolence wouldn't bring him the punishment he deserves...." and, in a postdata, the divine master told the divine bandit, "If you do it right I have prepared a large canvas for you, magnificently framed."

How could Aretino not comply with the request? He was a collector of masterpieces from the supreme masters, whom he praised, but when he tired of a specific piece, or needed a wall for a new acquisition, he put into practice Titian's advice and sold at an extremely high price. These operations involved ambassadors who arrived in Venice, Florence or Rome to purchase paintings for their kings. Aretino knew enough to take them to Titian's palace where he had a magnificent collection of Venetian women, superb experts in the art of convincing with their songs, smiles, delicious caresses and performances on the laud or the spinet, charged the master with the task of creating more works, marvels from his brush. These works, apart from delighting the universe and pumping up the ambassadors with shows of generosity from the genius, permitted Aretino to buy stupendous steeds, dazzling jewels and costumes so he could ride side by side with emperors and prelates, putting beyond doubt his excellence as a poet and his indisputable authority as an art critic.

Rivera continues exposing the art business with clarity and sincerity; a business where a curious multitude of psychological factors move their tentacles as in an aquarium around the great ocean of beauty. We find ourselves presently in the shoddy workshops of Mrs. Abraham and Levi, folk who wear sharkskin headwear. We enter a vast bedroom decorated as if by Balzac, where Princess Mona Lisa tries to smile while a miserable fly is stuck to her cheek. But let's get to the point:

In order to understand with clarity and precision any analysis dealing with the functioning of this business of art dealers, their collective and individual nature, and of the economic and social importance (meaning political) that this traffic has in the modern world, we have to look carefully to see who these characters are.

First off, we must refer to their relation to the providers (the artists and craftsmen), the presenters (critics), investigators (doctors in aesthetics, philosophy and letters), and in general, all those persons connected with the machinery of evaluation, exhibition, and acquisition made by public and private entities of works of art. We must refer to the consumers, the private and official collectors (governments, museum directors and all manner of fine art institutes), the eventual buyers (in consultation with all kinds of propagandists) plus the general public which, though it may not buy, forms on the other hand the masses that, by admiring, valuing and envying the purchasers, push them to acquire expensive objects and raise their position in society.

We must not forget the buyer seeking personal satisfaction. This rare type, not too numerous, can be found among all the strata mentioned before.

The business of the art dealer functions in two ways when earnings are made from the surplus value of the artist's work: first, from an actual sale. The dealer pays the agreed amount in cash and acquires all rights to the painting, at times including agreements for subsequent productions. This allows the dealer, when convenient, to draw public attention to the artist or bury the work in his warehouse waiting for his fame to grow. And what is even better, that the artist die after he is famous in which case what he acquired for 10 can be easily sold for 100, 10,000, or 100,000.

Paintings by Van Gogh, Cézanne and Picasso were bought by merchants for 3, 5, or 1,000 francs and sold for 20 and 30,000 dollars (or several million francs). If one had estimated the value of the franc as opposed to the dollar at the time of the sale, the painting bought for 1,000 francs would have been sold again for 50,000 francs, a gain of 500 percent.

Let me give you a concrete example from our own turf: A few years ago, while visiting the studio of José Clemente Orozco, his friend and colleague Carmen Mondragón asked José Clemente to give her a canvas from his first epoch that was rolling around on the floor doubled up in fourths and cracked, and such was the master's interest in her that he answered laughingly, "Okay, take it!" A few years later, Carmen, in spite of having enough talent herself to compare with a dozen painters she knew, fell in the most horrible misery, with no more bread than her books of poetry and essays, and with less flesh to her bones than the few cats that eventually came to be caught and cooked as rabbit stew. Forgotten by her former admirers who used to surround her like flies around honey in her years of splendid beauty, even by those who were or had wanted to be her husbands, one day of tremendous necessity she had to take the Orozco canvas to the gallery of don Alberto Misrachi. Because he admired Orozco and the seller, he gave her eight hundred pesos for it. Naturally, he had the painting restored and kept it in back of his store patiently for a few years, until one day he sold it for eight thousand dollars! And look, after Orozco's death, since the piece was an extremely rare example of the master's early painting style, he could have easily sold it for 15 or 20,000 dollars. This last didn't happen because our friend Misrachi isn't really a *'marchant de tableaux'* but is instead involved, as all Mexico knows, in selling books, magazines, fountain pens and other desk items which normally don't bring such an extraordinary rise in price when their makers die.

Secondly: The works of an artist can be obtained on commission. There exists a tacit international convention that allows for the commission to be one third of the price the artist asks for his work, the famous 33.33 percent. This system is not followed by dealers of great reputation and capital except with artists they are not sure of, yet want to try out with the public.

They might also choose to use such works as a *'repoussoir,'* an object that disgusts the client and pushes him, in reaction, to acquire another more convenient for the dealer. Also such works are used, as the slang of dealers has it, to play the role of 'rugs' or 'tapestries,' providing an adequate background to highlight objects bought for cash and sell them quicker.

It is quite easy to understand that through both gambits, the merchant is interested in orienting the opinion and taste of his customers; for this, he shamelessly underwrites magazines advertising his gallery, paying a lot. Such magazines can freely ask for articles or accept them, employing those critics whose tendencies lean toward the dealer that underwrites not just the magazine but the critic honestly selling his articles.

Contrary to what you might imagine, my dear Cardona Peña, art dealers no longer have crooked noses, though one or two might still conserve one out of coquetry. In reality, there are ladies and gentlemen of the most varied of ethnographic backgrounds involved. And among us '*nous soit dit*' that the Jews are precisely the least greedy and better informed, without in the least having this deny the just renown enjoyed by the illustrious Bernheim, Cassirer, Kantwheiller, Rosenberg and other families.

The king of those dealing with Impressionism was the totally 100 percent French Monsieur Durand-Rueil, who made great deals with the help of an art critic, art philosopher, collector, and man of the world. Theodore Duret, as French as the other, was also helped by personages distant from Jewish blood as Monsieur le Marquis de Magallon d'Argent. This last was an admirer and backer of another noble genius, though deformed due to a fall from a horse due to the impertinence of his father, who wanted to make him a rider worthy of his blood. That idiot father was Count Toulouse-Lautrec; his child genius Henri de Toulouse-Lautrec.

The most interesting and powerful personage among the *marchants de tableaux* was monsieur Ambroise Vollard, not because of his money (which he earned in the millions), but due to his talent and original way of functioning. His good sense of smell allowed him to guess, from among the most vilified and discarded painters of his time, those who would rise to the top of their generation. Vollard was the biographer, friend, model and dealer of the enormous master Cézanne, besides being an anti-Semite in the *Action Francaise*. For his own good and gain, he had confidence in Toulouse-Lautrec just as the Marquis de Magallon felt towards Renoir, Van Gogh, *et les plus jeunes de tous,* Henri Matisse and Pablo Picasso.

At a time when the very Emile Zola looked down on his friend Cézanne, with all his contemporaries considering him a "*raté*," Vollard began by making friends with Cézanne, and presented the master and his work to some highly placed politicians such as Clemenceau. He glanced over the shoulders of those deifying Manet, Claude Monet, Pizarro, and even the same Renoir, to acquire practically the entire *oeuvre* of Cézanne, paying whatever came to mind. Then he organized the first exhibition of his friend in Paris, renting the fine gallery of Durand-Raeil. And when some politically important friend took the master to see his own exposition, the master took one look at the vast salon and exclaimed, "*Ce patan Vollard, il a tout encadré!*" (That bastard Vollard, he has framed everything)

Those marvelous paintings, true works of art of the XIX century, which nobody wanted even for free, were sometimes thrown away into the top of trees or left forgotten in the bushes by Cézanne because the master was interested in the pleasure of painting, in finding what he was looking for. By the time he had a small court of knowing friends, these would take excursions in the country frequented by the master with the object of looking for and at times finding some silvan Cézanne. Today, those pieces couldn't be purchased for less than 60 to 100,000 dollars.

The first friend Vollard conquered for Cézanne was a rich margarine maker from Sweden, who was something of a consul to France. That king of Swedish margarine was monsieur Pellerin, who had a hotel near the Champs Élysées and, in it, the most marvelous collection of Cézannes imaginable. It had all come from Ambroise Vollard and included The Card Players, The Bathers, and other immortal paintings. But the funny part was that Vollard kept for himself paintings with the same titles but of better quality.

The Pellerin collection became famous throughout the world, and when one of its pieces had to be sold, something originally purchased for 20,000 francs and already an exorbitant price for that time and at the height of Cézanne's fame, was sold for two and even three million francs. Those 'doubles' of Vollard found in American collections, once their quality had been found to be equal or superior to those in the Pellerin collection, have been sold for 600,000, 800,000 and even for 1,200,000 dollars!

The same thing happened with the paintings of another disregarded artist of his time, the marvelous pointilist master Georges Seurat. His widow roofed some chicken coops with some of those paintings, they were that hard to sell. Years later Dr. Barnes, of Philadelphia, the billionaire, acquired one of the paintings that had failed to make it to the chicken coop roof, thanks to the fact that it had been bought by Monsieurs Bernheim and Co. on the advice of the anarchist critic Charles Fencon. The Bernheims were Jews resembling English gentlemen, and the anarchist Fenton, descendant from a well-to-do family, had the wit to present himself as an ashaverus, including a jewel on his head just to mock his patrons and clients.

The Bernheim gentlemen 'generously' acquired Seurat's Bathers for 3,200 francs and sold it 'modestly' to Mr. Barnes for 980,000 dollars.

Monsieur Ambroise Vollard, who wasn't Jewish like Bernheim, purchased, according to Picasso himself (who told me this one afternoon when I had taken him to my studio to look at my work) that Ambroise's employees had taken every painting from his studio at the Rue Ravignan for 5,000 francs in three carts. Figure at least fifty paintings in each cart. We have to note that these were paintings from his blue, rose, Lautrec, Cézannist and analytical Cubism periods and that today, Picasso's blue period is the most expensive and most sought after. One could not buy an important painting of that period, taken by Vollard by the cartload, for less than 20 to 30,000 francs.

When Picasso became famous at last, Vollard wanted to compensate him generously for that huge affair and told the painter, "paint my portrait." And so, during his analytical period when he was enduring the worst criticism, Picasso did Vollard, scandalizing the world of art and the dealers' trade union chamber. Vollard gave Picasso some 30,000 francs in, I believe, a cigarette case which, in one blow, raised the 5,000 Vollard had invested initially at the price level set by the chamber, to a minimum of 4,500,000 francs. The convention among those dealers was that if a member raised a certain type of work to such and such a level, the others had to accept that level for anything they might own. The one setting the new price is obligated to rescue the fellow who set the original level of so and so to his level. In the same way, if a private holder of such work presents it for sale to the dealers, these are obligated to pay the amount that has been set. In this way fabulous stock operations are carried out subject to the rise and fall of value plus possible panics. In this give and take the money ends up with the speculators. Remember our proverb that says, "From one month to the next, the cash belongs to the bush-whacker."

I was forgetting to add that just as the Wall Street bandits have their Wall Street Journal, the outlaws of the *Chambre Syndicale des Marchands* have their newspaper—*Les Arts*—in Paris, a shameless bulletin addressed to collectors, speculators and knowledgeable buyers called *gogos* in Paris and suckers in the United States.

Rivera has explained, with his golden beak and his falcon's eye the psychological and financial phenomena behind La Chambre Syndicale, *the workings of the stock market which raises the price of a certain work to the stratosphere. Now we are going to appreciate the opposite function, in other words, the depreciation of aesthetic values, since in this traffic, value goes up and down all the time, like the temperature of a man with malaria.*

To gain from a lowering of a stock value, dealers pick artists who produce a lot and who, according to the language of the game, have "flooded the market." The members of the Chamber and its sidekicks have taken part in that flood. And when the painter, an abundant producer, doesn't die in time and can't stop the amount of his output, the banking investment, the upkeep of the value of his work, is in danger and in that case it is preferable to play low.

There are always interests pro and con regarding the same level of artistic production as to how to capitalize on loss. The dealers talk to the critics and to experts with an aesthetic opposite that of the painter whose work is being devalued. The theories of those opposed to the painter are approved, and articles are asked for in magazines controlled by the dealers; doubts are raised with collectors, patrons and patronesses of art. The big dealers drop disparaging references about the artist, and finally it is resolved to lower prices to a minimum extreme in the Chamber, realizing in this way the first part of their offensive. Next comes a public auction. This helps to take the public pulse as to its maturity or immaturity regarding the drop in value and that is why the *marchands* don't posture when offering each other the works that are about to go down in price. If the public makes offers, the offensive stops and a new auction is improvised, with no publicity, and where a few miserable souls, paid by the dealers, speak ill of the artist, making sure they are heard by the audience so that when the man's work is offered at auction, they let it fall to the minimum extreme decided upon previously, which is the one the dealers used to purchase the work before all the maneuvering. Critiques are reinforced and commentaries are made regarding the low prices, not only in the art magazines, but in those of a large circulation. Now we have a panic among the holders of auction-bought paintings. Logically, the fright is on the part of those who have purchased the art through the big dealers, so they hurry to take back the works to those sellers. The wolves, gnashing their teeth and using the opportunity to truly attack the under-valued paintings, return the money. There are owners who can't return work to the *marchand* who sold it to them and they try all kinds of maneuvers to get rid of it. This makes the panic grow. And this is the time when the businessmen begin to buy the work twice and three times bought and sold paying the prices they paid the painter. They retire them from circulation, so they remain in the hands of the members of the Chamber. These possess the capital that constitutes the difference between the initial price and the successive ones, not only the high, but the low.

I will cite a concrete example: In 1921, a painting by Chirico could be acquired by a *marchand* like Paul Guillon for 500 francs if it was a canvas size 14, or for 1,000 if it was 20 or 25 in size. Towards 1935 or 36, those paintings Guillon had bought were selling for 350,000 francs. Others did the same. Chirico continued to produce and evolve. Towards 1937 or 38 he quarreled with the surrealists, who had previously heralded him as their flag bearer. In consequence, he was attacked by the critics from that party. The businessmen immediately took advantage and gave great assistance to the attacks and limited or silenced any manifestation of defense. The panic started and it has been growing to such a degree that paintings once sold for 250,000 or 450,000 are being sold actually for 150 to 250 dollars, which represent a fourth of the cost, in spite of the fact that in the epoch of Chirico's success a dollar was worth 50 francs and today 450. So now those businessmen got work whose prices they had previously raised, five times lower than originally. Today those paintings have been put away in the hope that they will lose even more value (while the knowing public today has begun to react and be upset by such loses). Within three or five years a well selected exposition, with the critics on hand, will bring attention again to a painter by then ignored. An auction will follow and the big shots, hitting their breasts, will acquire the disdained paintings for large sums. This will be all the easier if by then Chirico has died. If that is the case, the collectors and fans who got rid of the work during the panic, will come back looking for them. The gain game will begin, and for each underestimated painting, a little bitty amount of money will enter the coffers of the dealers once again.

6

MEXICAN PAINTING

Why does great Mexican art exist? What causes determined the appearance of that plastic phenomenon known as the Mexican Renaissance in this country and not in another?

Painting is an essential function of human life. Wherever human beings live, painting has existed and exists. Painting is a language, as with words. I must tell you that when it comes to the Mexican Renaissance occurring here, the matter has highly complex historical causes which, by the way, haven't been clearly analyzed up to this day by anybody. These are:

A/ The marvelous plastic tradition of Anahuac. In the pre-Hispanic world everything in the life of the people was artistic, from the palaces and temples which are monumental works of sculpture, with their magnificent frescoes that amaze everyone peering at them in the jungle, down to the most humble pot used daily, and the children's toys, and the stone to grind grain. Everything was a work of art, ninety-nine percent of the time, a masterpiece.

The pre-Hispanic peoples were artistic peoples, including the lives they led where there was an uninterrupted development of masterpieces, from death in the fields to flowering war. The oppression they felt, the iniquity of tribute, did not interrupt or diminish the superior quality of people's lives. Their socio-pyramidal hierarchy made excessively easy the decapitation of painters, just as the fine nature of Mexican art made possible their defeat before men able to withstand being cooked alive in the sweat, filth, and disease within the iron shells of their armatures. The horseman was more resistant but less capable of appreciating the beauty of Anahuac than the beast he was mounted on.

Three hundred years of suppression of the plastic genius of the Aztecs (achieved through the rule of the rodents of the Inquisition of the Holy Office) were not enough to completely destroy that incomparable example of vitality. It became necessary for the Spaniards to preserve the Indians because, as opposed to the Anglo Saxons and the French, they didn't come to work the land with their own hands but to have the Indian slaves work for them. The phrase used by the great Cabeza de Vaca, named that for obvious reasons, was, "to move forward benefiting from war." I also recall marvelous Bernal Díaz del Castillo saying, "We told them we had a mortal ailment that could only be cured with gold, and they brought us a great quantity thereof...."

That was the disadvantage those artists of that time encountered versus valiant adventurers.

B/ That sleeping tradition, limited during the Colony to reproducing religious images and to make at times admirable and often extraordinary portraits and still lives, revived when Mexico achieved its independence. But this didn't take place on lordly walls, whose owners only looked toward Europe, nor on government edifices since those governing, except for the enormous

Juarez, were not even aware of their imbecility, and went on looking for their owners outside the country. It only came to life where it could, in taverns, greasy spoons, inns and cheap hotels, as well as in some rural churches where, as in grocery stores, it could manifest its former, not entirely dead, plastic genius. This talent continued alive as well in those transformed manifestations of the pre-Hispanic world which our pedantic, idiotic intellectuals call "popular arts" with a suave smile and a hint of disdain.

C/ When in 1910 the people *en masse* chose to die of hunger and thirst in battles and skirmishes rather than on the pallets of the haciendas and in the infected hovels of workers in the cities, when so many foremen and overseers of opportunistic *tinacal* (?) turned into liberating generals, when so many petty bourgeois namby-pambies wore the uniform of the General Staff of the landed estates, turning into petty bosses that would later aid Anglo-Saxon imperialism in its task of robbing the people whose only sin had been to sacrifice two million souls of their own, then the people, from the days of Posada until now, chose to use their own intrinsic expression: graphics, since Mexicans already wrote, thought, poeticized, and managed their social activities through all kinds of works of art. Thanks to the Revolution, the people regained their own language and spoke through the receptors that were capable of capturing, condensing and re-transmitting the popular voice.

D/ The receptors, condensers and re-transmitters had a capable structure and function since they were able to activate an effective theory and practice with primary Mexican materials. What is this struggle? To work to bring about a truly human society by the destruction of the capitalist world and thus build a new one that will not be divided into classes. In other words, that the machines (the artists) at the service of the Mexican people were built by the engineers of that new society. Marx, Engels, and Joseph Stalin. This last factor was decisive so that Mexico, and no other place on the continent, could produce that phenomenon traditionally named in art history the "Mexican Renaissance."

When Mexican painting began to interest the public on an international basis, back in 1923 or thereabouts, some dealers in New York looked into it as a source for business.

A book by Walter Pach entitled *Masters of Modern Art* had appeared which included a chapter on my work, from my cubist period down to the murals in the first patio of the Secretary of Public Education. While speaking of my painting, he referred in general to the importance that the present art of Mexico was acquiring.

Soon after appeared the books by Ana Brenner, *Idols Behind Altars* and *The Mexican Renaissance*. Many critical articles began to appear in the US, Europe, and South America dealing with the work of José Clemente Orozco and my own, in which they were already speaking about the new plastic movement in Mexico. The gallery Dudensing in New York, through the artist Miguel Covarrubias, contacted artists here, offering us their showrooms to present our work. A similar offer through Anita Brenner was made by the Matisse gallery in New York, signing up Emilio Sala, the Spanish painter who was part of our group. There was another agreement with Covarrubias to present his work without a commitment to buy it, merely to sell it, if they could find clients for it. But we Mexican painters were sufficiently excited about the new, social sense of mural painting and didn't respond to the invitation. We were all lacking sufficient time to work on walls, done under disastrous economic conditions. Surely, never have muralists been worse paid than we were then, nor so badly cursed and insulted as we were. Nevertheless, not one among us thought for a minute to change that rocky and thorny road for the velvet carpet path implied by them.

Second and third-rate painters heard that siren song and organized expositions in New York but found little success and, since the dealers felt they had failed to attract the main artists, they didn't continue, figuring that Mexican painting was out of control. Besides, the public attention directed toward muralism was a real threat for the bandits of the Trade Chamber and the agents living off them as peddlers of their wares. From that first moment, they prepared to attack, but public interest in the new stage Mexican painters had begun in the world was such that they could not derail it. The dealers waited, trying to undermine the ground.

This new worldwide public interest in Mexican mural painting did not rest, as some believe or pretend to believe nowadays, in that the work involved encaustic, or al fresco techniques nor on murals per se. In Europe and in the United States itself, they had been painting murals. The official saloons in Paris were annually loaded with enormous canvasses meant to be hung on government and private walls. That production was not less abundant in Italy, Germany, Austria, or even Switzerland, where Ferdinand Hodler, a muralist of international fame, resided. In the Scandinavian countries you had one of great quality in Munch.

The true novelty of Mexican painting which I initiated in 1922–23 at the Secretary of Public Education, along with Siqueiros and Orozco in the National Preparatory School, was to make the people the heroes of mural painting; it consisted in representing the poor farmer and the industrial worker fighting to obtain land.

This had certain European antecedents in the sculpture of Constantin Meunier, the great Belgian master, as well as in

Munch's painting, but in both cases the worker was seen as a spectacle of great plastic beauty (sometimes even glorified), but they didn't have a class sense; precisely, not one of class struggle. For the first time in the history of art, Mexican art achieved that. Up to then, the heroes of murals had been gods, angels, archangels, saints, heroes of war, kings and emperors, prelates, great military and political chiefs, with the people showing up, even in the best cases, as the chorus around the stellar personages of the tragedy. Even Soviet painting prior to this time was like that. Parallel to our appearance here they had their own episodes with the October revolution, but they didn't concretize it, as we did here with the mass-hero. This only took place in the USSR towards 1926–27. This is the glory, in reality, of Mexican mural painting which, by 1929, manifested its social and classic direction in the frescos of the stairway at the National Palace. In them, for the first time in the history of art a painting was realized which, on a single wall expressed dialectically the history of a people from the remote past (including its mythological aspect) up to the present in order to establish a perspective about the future from a criteria connected to the historical materialism of Marx, Engels, Lenin and Stalin.

This happening sounded a definite alert, not only to dealers in painting, but to capitalist society in its most powerful and representative nucleus, the North American bourgeoisie.

Just as today that bourgeoisie spends thousands of millions to stop the march of history, that is to say, the arrival of scientific socialism, in 1929, it sought to detain the historic march of revolutionary painting, inviting Mexican painters to paint for it in the United States. We went there, José Clemente Orozco, and I, and the results obtained by their attempt to get something, were the anti-imperialist murals of Orozco at Dartmouth College, and of

Siqueiros in Los Angeles, as was my mural at Rockefeller Center. In that work I was able to place, around the image of Lenin, a historical perspective that included the war just past. In the center of the composition a worker appears in control of world equilibrium, and a human hand holds a transparent sphere within which is a sketch of the much-ballyhooed hydrogen bomb, with uranium as the detonator. Of course, the work was destroyed, but restored in Mexico, a failure of capitalism, which attempted to silence the happenings that are today one hundred percent confirmed. This event determined the actual offensive against Mexican painting, and we should pause to consider its existence.

To understand this offensive well, we must clearly analyze who are the enemies that integrate it, otherwise an exposition of the facts will be confusing. Naturally, beneath all their reasons and motives, there is an economic cause, but the way to understand that, nourishing the roots till we get to the trunk, the branches, leaves, flowers and fruit, is quite different for each kind of enemy one can group into species, families and subfamilies, as with the mineral and vegetal worlds.

The enemies are from outside and inside the country. The foreigners are not always the worst. Often, they are employed by those on the inside, and that is one of the most curious things about our phenomenon. In my own case my worst enemies have been local. To initiate their offensive, above all when they belong routinely to what are called friends and social acquaintances, they rely on foreigners who remain that or become Mexican nationals on their own accord or have been born here from foreign parents.

Thus, from the days of a magazine called *Contemporaneos,* which used a Spaniard, Mr. García Maroto, the attacks transmigrated to *El Hijo Pródigo*, the attacks were not just against me but what was much worse, against José Guadalupe Posada and José

María Velasco, whose greatness as a painter is above any other, if one considers painting as a constructive creation through color. In order to attack Posada, these small-minded locals and weak *mestizos* employed another Spaniard named Ramoncito Gaya (not *gallo,* rooster). And to honor very honorable but lesser artists, Mr. José Bergamín tried to undermine the greatness of Velasco. A person of dignified background and solid critical background, Ms. Margarita Nelken, attacked Mexican art in the most voluminous and substantive current magazine, Cuadernos Americanos. As for a national enemy, I can cite the eminent autodidact don Enrique Erro.

The reasons for such actions have different bases, though, all of them, as I have said, are of an economic origin. Often, those roots are hard to perceive even if one digs in front of the plant. Of course, no matter how subtle, they are ultimately obvious. In more than half the cases, the economic roots of the offensive apply to all the social classes of Mexican society. The reason for this is the semi-colonial condition, at the economic level, of all our Ibero-American countries which, as we all know, lack a national, independent economy, including the more developed of them. Lacking proper economic independence, it is impossible to have true political independence and without both, there is no cultural independence, leading to an epic comic, ridiculous situation.

It consists in this. The basic strata of our peoples, especially those closest to the earth due to the characteristics of their agrarian class, conserve bits of the marvelous pre-Iberian culture, bits all the deeper and evident the more distant they are from the urban-colonial centers of yesterday and the semi-colonial ones of the present day. As a logical consequence, this state of things is true among that population that we—a shameful monstrosity—continue to call Indian or indigenous thanks to our lack of identity and national unity.

Those entities that we here call middle and upper classes, and which name themselves managing classes upon entering a wider economy, are caught by the forces of that economy they joined. Those forces do not reside in the Indo-American nations, but in the capitals of the great capitalist countries which export their capital to us.

In reality, this situation converts our so-called managing classes into simple intermediaries and, let's state it frankly, into salesmen and overseers at the service of those powerful, rich and potent foreign bourgeoisies who impose the buying price of our own products, and sell us theirs. We are obligated to consume what they produce, and determine for our money the diminished worth convenient to them, reducing our wealthy heads of state into the servants of foreign capital. They either capitalize on the money of their outside bosses (which handicaps them to a huge proportion relative to the great lords of finance), or forces them to depend on the exchange value imposed by the exterior power. He who was a Mexican millionaire when the exchange was four pesos per dollar, is no longer a millionaire today when the dollar is where it is. In the same way, many of our nine thousand millionaires who are that in Mexico by having from three to seven million pesos, are not millionaires of any sort in the United States.

Such a state of things bring out in the Indo-Ibero-American petty bourgeoisie an irremediable inferiority complex which we must more accurately call a semi-colonial inferiority complex because it translates into an attitude of anxiousness to appear to be like their foreign masters.

In that way, the Indo-Ibero-American sub-bourgeoisie ends up believing that it is a life and death question to universalize itself, and they call that the act of imitating the owners of large foreign capital, just like the servants of wealthy houses imitate their superiors when these are away on vacation, putting on their fancy clothes of the evening and serving themselves formal meals after abandoning the kitchen for the dining room.

This economic attitude, which could greatly inform comic and dramatic literature, but which our writers ignore, does immense harm to us at the level of culture.

Since our Indo-Ibero-American managing classes do not possess the means of study equal to those they try to imitate, they create here, especially in countries as poor as Mexico, a pseudo-culture similar but third rate. Our men of culture attempt to leap over the heads of their imperialist bosses to get to the sources of their culture. This explains how the biggest majority of our men of letters feel they are Latin from the epoch of the Republic or that of the Caesars, or Hellenics from Pericles' time, or even from previous mythical times prior to the Trojan war, and are immensely delighted when some friend photographs them, changing their brown eyes to blue, and whatever hair they had from dark to blonde.

This is how all literary, philosophical, and artistic production is tinged with this aspiration to be white and blond; it also generates an ignorance, sometimes total, of historical circumstances, permitting them to ignore what is before their eyes night and day, and bringing up in them an almost instinctive horror for whatever has its own native characteristics. This attitude induced the group, Contemporaries, to have Mr. Maroto "demonstrate" through his critique how my painting contains foreign elements, something which tranquilizes them in their own condition. That same reason propelled the picturesque Gaya against Posada, one hundred percent Mexican, and scoundrels to go against the greatest among us, Master José María Velasco. The same thing determined that my very old acquaintance Margarita Nelken would attempt to ingratiate herself with those who had been *contemporaneos* twenty years ago. Apparently, everything in me was borrowed from the Parisian school, for the peace of mind and clear conscience of those functioning editors who collaborate in French in *La Société des Critíques d'art* in the pages of the magazine *Les Arts*, the official syndicate of the *marchands de tableaux*, as already mentioned, no different from the Wall Street Journal. Because the dealers in paintings have their francs down to 450 per dollar, they should be interested—and how they are!—in Mexican pesos going for nine to the dollar, and much, oh so much more than our pleasant (how not!) incipient collectors.

The relation between francs and pesos with the dollar is the most important reason for the foreign campaign against Mexican painting, especially against mural painting, which is the one with the greatest national character up to now. It also explains the reason why they handle paintings by Mexicans, which, though having good intrinsic qualities, resemble foreign ones and get sold as ultra-modern work by the thieves of the Syndical Chamber.

The first to do this kind of painting was Vasily Kandinsky, its great master around 1900, followed in 1908 by Paul Klee. Around that time, Picasso, utilizing elements from Cézanne's constructions of objective planes, and those of Seurat through spacial planes, besides black and pre-Hispanic American sculpture, essayed cubism with extraordinary success. Picasso had already announced this style in his Black American neo-Cézannism of 1907. He had encountered pieces of black sculpture and our own pre-Hispanic items in the Trocadero Museum and in antique shops in Paris.

But so-called abstractionism only reached France in 1913 with Marcel Duchamp, a great painter, with the Dutch artist Piet Mondrian and a few others. All these, eight years after Kandinsky had initiated the movement followed by Paul Klee, by the American Lyonel Feininger and the Russian Pole Jawlensky. [The ethnicity for Mondrian and Feininger, and nationality and spelling for Jawlensky have been corrected in this edition. —Edit.] These formed "the four blues," denominated this way by a book in which Kandinsky outlined his theory of abstractionism in painting. Basically, this theory was realistic since it re-vindicated in painting the right to use forms and colors, qualities and profundities in the same sway musicians use sound; in other words, creating a musical reality parallel to but not reflecting the physical world of sound.

This position, which has everything but abstraction in it (it isn't for nothing that Kandinsky was an excellent professor of economy at Moscow University), was distorted and falsified by the critics at the service of the *marchands de tableaux* with the object of creating a critical poetic smokescreen so the public would swallow and pay for the merchandise they sold. And since the most important thing was (according to that deep sea diver, Papini) to dream in front of a piece of cardboard or cloth covered in color even if the public couldn't figure out what it was looking at. On the other hand, since no fan will declare himself or herself incapable of dreaming (since there's nothing more chic than dreaming), who could resist the elegant gesture of paying many dollars for the patent of being a big dreamer?

I would want a statement of yours regarding dreaming, that two-edged sword.

With great pleasure. Look here, dreaming is expensive; it's a merchandise that involves the imagination, and all this kind of thing is extremely more expensive in the present capitalist order as opposed to digestion. In poetry, which is a dream for dreamers, there are, as you told me once, a great quantity of active principles for living, all of which, my dear Cardona, makes me recall that life is made up of vigilance and the oneiric. This means that dreams and daydreams are a terribly important source of nourishment for the nervous system; they have a decisive influence on the actions of the awakened. Briefly, art and poetry have existed since man defined himself as such on the surface of this ball we call Earth.

Unfortunately, the word dreamer has been discredited, and some poets who have betrayed poetry see it like a slap in the face.

Really, some fear they will be called dreamers when their actual mission is that. If they didn't have it, they wouldn't have the gift of prediction, consequently losing almost all their usefulness. But just as it is easy to set a price for wheat, meat or beans, all foods for the digestive system, it is most difficult to set up tariffs for the food of the nervous or emotional systems. That is why, with the instinct to preserve, there is a tacit intelligence between producers and those who deal in aesthetic emotions (all manner of critics can be included in that second category). To wit: poetry, fictional prose or florid romances, music, architecture, painting, sculpture, drawing, film, dance, mimic representations, photography, etc., all of them, as a whole, are diverse forms of the poetic continent which is, as you can see, the merchandise that involves the imagination. This is sold at a higher rate, though with less economic advantage, especially for poets, who are the most terribly exploited among us. We can say, with the possible exception of Aretino who demanded good doubloons, and that of José Santos Chocano, of whom Carlos Pellicer said precisely in a letter addressed to you, that he was "an enormous poet and a big scoundrel," demanding the government to pay him 30,000 soles for his chant to Peru.

We mustn't forget that the gift of martyrdom brings us glory, and that glory brings certain compensations on this earth, precisely those that mortals who aren't poets, neither by word or sound, form or color, pay an extraordinarily high price to compensate for what we can only purchase with the poetry we can come up with. And since in this life, from the mineral to the most beautiful of women, the supreme activity is love, and since love—as Ovid told us—is an art and art technique, we are professional technicians.

Professional businessmen have found a Mexican example in Rufino Tamayo, a painter of great talent, naming him a relative of Picasso, Chagall, and Klee to sell him as something opposite to our Mexican novo-realistic movement, which is capable of blowing away with its vital breath any kind of smoke screen.

Such stupendous stuff made of dreams and dollars!

Yes, but when we Mexican muralists penetrated the United States, there was alarm among painting dealers and they mobilized their agents. The North-American bourgeoisie opened museums and markets for abstract art but since it didn't know how to praise our work, began to buy it in silence.

The gag to silence us was called, poetically, purist art and abstractionism.

From that moment on, they tried to get the market of North-American art to get rid of Mexican art so they bought all Picasso imitators like the Mexican Tamayo and certain Cubans which to the Yankee brain looked all the same.

Galleries and the private showrooms of snobs were closed to us.

The slogan we had adopted, "art for the masses," going back to the October Revolution, was now a reality and the great North-American public shrugged its shoulders and continued buying the paintings which were supposed to be eliminated from the market.

I can assure you that I have sold more paintings to individuals I have never met in the United States after that offensive than before. Some have come here exclusively to have me paint their portraits. Dealers, critics and aesthetic investigators at their service haven't stopped their offensive attempts, notably because in Mexico, thanks to favorable circumstances after the last war, sufficient capital has been accumulated to invest, even if minimally, in art.

Some rich industrialists from here began to purchase paintings; so much so that during the first two wartime years I had no time to sell any important painting to foreign clients except portraits. My work was acquired by new collectors from here, often specially commissioned.

The same happened to José Clemente Orozco and later to David Alfaro Siqueiros. Then markets in New York and Paris began to dream they could find an innocent and easy market in Mexico for what they sell.

There was a massive immigration of antique furniture, upholstery, Sévres porcelain, and old paintings. They even risked sending a few modern ones of indisputable reputation, like Renoir and Courbet, slipping in one or two Picassos, Chiricos, and María Laurencins.

The first landing on Mexican shores was commanded by Mr. Aquabella, a member of the famous Syndical Chamber of Paris, with the help of Mr. Alberto Misrachi and the unconscious intervention in good faith of our friend the poet Carlos Pellicer, who imagined seeing masterworks of art everywhere.

Pellicer saw works from the old world in the collection of Mr. Aquabella, who managed to put on a show of moth-eaten paintings right in the main hall of the National Palace of Bellas Artes and in that of a white Russian who, being Russian and all, was frank enough to tell me that he wasn't more than a speculator working under the grandiose pseudonym of Koenigsber.

When Aquabella arrived, he wanted to ingratiate himself with Mexican painters so they wouldn't groan too much. He tried to begin with me and arrived at my studio with Alberto Misrachi as the go-between with ambassadors, looking to succeed since Misriachi had sold many of my paintings with constructive benefit for himself.

At that moment I was working on a painting for Jacques Gelman, an associate of my friend Misrachi through Posa Films and a film producer or the actor Cantinflas. I was also doing the portrait of a beautiful friend, wife of the principal banker of a king in exile, probably a morganatic daughter. Immediately, *il caballieri* Aquabella made me some dishonest proposals regarding the paintings I was working on, involving substantial dollars. Since I wouldn't take the bait, the Aquabella-Misrachi entity took another path, no longer to Diego but to Villadiego. [Rivera refers here to a Spanish saying about getting away quickly from some danger: *coger las de Villadiego*. —Trans.]

A few days later some articles appeared in one of Mexico's big dailies penned by an anonymous psychiatrist (everyone knows that in Mexico we have psychiatrists for every ailment), declaring that Diego Rivera, Orozco, and Siqueiros were crazy. This is how dealers in old paintings (of which those that were old had nine-tenths of their surfaces retouched, and the others were simply disguised or false copies) hoped to invalidate the opinions of the best-known painters in Mexico. They knew that we wouldn't hesitate to let the public that had made money during the war know they were out to drain their funds with old paintings that weren't worth a penny. Nevertheless, in spite of the gross means employed, thanks to the freedom that exists to rob, cheat, and insult in print, the success of that *foire aux croutes* was much less than the extractors of cash to be taken out of the country from the newly rich expected.

Only a few innocents, among them a great dealer in water tanks and plumbing materials who choked on a "Veronese," fell for this *piece a cons.*

The most conspicuous, though less rich than others involved, was the great man of American photography, the admirable Alfred Stieglitz, who, as so many other North American artists, had been born in Germany. Others were born in Poland, Hungary, Chekoslovakia, France, many from Russia, but the mighty dollar ultimately nationalizes everyone. However, I believe that the resultant nationality is inconvenient, especially in this atomic age.

Alfred Stieglitz was the first to sell and collect my paintings in the United States. They were from my cubist period naturally, twenty-five years ago, when cubism wasn't a familiar item in the Americas and not in vogue as it is today.

Alfred didn't attack me or Orozco, but did attack those American painters who had been influenced by Mexican muralism. In a matter of months, those painters had united themselves and begun to work, thanks to a government subsidy, which, on a trial basis, gave them no less than eight million dollars. That is equivalent to what we in Mexico would have made if we could have actively been at work for 500 years. Considering the wages we get paid by our supreme Federal government, and prices at the time, just after the Agua Prieta coup, we would have had to work all together, hard, no less than 3,000 years. The one making the most at the time was I, enjoying the splendid earnings, in Mexican money, of what would be two dollars and fifty cents for each square meter painted. To earn eight million dollars, we Mexicans would have had to paint much more than 3,500,000 square meters.

Stieglitz called that movement, provoked by us, the "Mexican Disease," recalling the Spanish influenza epidemic that caused so many deaths during WWI and our Revolution here.

But the thing didn't go beyond an underground and a mute resistance, as well as the mobilizing of certain critics, against us. But that was precisely the moment when our movement grew and one saw murals springing up everywhere.

But the State, wanting to make the deal larger so they could have "bigger and better murals," didn't manage to see a single mural in its favor because in all the North American territory there did not appear a single perverse, corruptible artist. Only a few foreigners played at it, like an Englishman by that name of Browning, who allowed them to buy him with dollars. But after that, the rules of the offensive against Mexican muralism and Mexicans sounded the attack clearly in all its forms.

I must tell you that among the enemies of Mexican painting in the world, not only have they made expeditions against us with old merchandise they call antique plus implied contemporaneousness they call modern. No. They have also meddled with our painting to try and depreciate it. That's why they organized a kind of sale of minor work, especially drawings and watercolors, by José Clemente Orozco and me, at Macy's, a bazaar, which, besides selling clothing and other stuff, has a so-called "art gallery." To carry out that offensive, they brought a Russian Jew specializing in that kind of trick. He tempted the collector Alberto Misrachi (easily tempted when things are in dollars), plus others who had our drawings and watercolors. I think he even showed an oil or a tempera or two. The show was announced on a whole page of the *Weekly Times* in such a way as to disgust all the high-fallutin' collectors, clients of the major dealers. There were unfaithful reproductions of our drawings in the *Times*, while the texts read, "Orozco and Rivera are in our time what Michelangelo was in the past. Are you going to pass up the chance to buy a Michelangelo for 30 dollars? You can acquire a drawing from one of these gigantic geniuses for that sum, and if you invest 80, 100, 200 or 300 dollars you can obtain an important work from one of them."

The fanfare was such that even Misrachi was pulling his hair, but in reality, save for one or two wealthy buyers (surely Mexican of the type that has business over there, on the other side) who complained of having stuff at home selling in New York bazaars, the coup was perfectly unsuccessful.

The art-for-art-sake galleries had already shut their doors on us long before. Neither Orozco nor I enjoyed the kind of public they did, but the only tangible result, since the situation didn't fail to cause me disgust due to its intention, was not to sell Misrachi anything for him to resell. This mattered little to him since he was up to other games.

A year after this plan, which must have appeared disgusting to the most conspicuous and well-known dealers of Paris and New York as far as contemporary painting is concerned, the famous *marchant* Rosenberg proposed to exhibit my work, which he would sell in his gallery. I accepted, since the painters in his gallery could not have been better (with Picasso at the head) but since, for a while, a public in Mexico had interested itself in Mexican painting to the point of acquiring it and paying for it as well as those holding dollars, I could never get together enough canvasses, water colors and drawings to have the show. I failed for three years in a row after having set the dates for it. Rosenberg finally got tired of waiting and we cancelled the project.

Also, American aficionados are interested in my work is spite of all those campaigns against me, including those of my beloved Mexican colleagues, who accuse me of painting exclusively for tourists since travelers from the States buy my work with more frequency than they do theirs. Nevertheless, those puny colleagues proffer their paintings with an insistence infinitely greater than mine, including using charming North American agents involving the three sexes.

Frequently, and this is something that didn't happen before, persons have come (the majority being collectors and clients of the big dealers who campaign against our work) to have their portraits painted by Orozco, Siqueiros, and I, as well as to buy other works.

When the commercial confabulations against us started to fail, another type of offensive was begun, but we mustn't forget that the biggest enemy of Mexican painting is not, when you come down to it, the dealer but someone much bigger, the class enemy, in other words, the politicians, the most reactionary sector of the high North American bourgeoisie, connected directly with the official apparatus there. These folks set up the most curious and touching offensive, so naïve in its attempt to work, believing they could con us here at home into mobilizing from our university professors down to ambassadors and men of science.

Among those ambassadors we must remember the deceased Dwight Morrow, who knew well the weaknesses of North American diplomats and early enough understood the character of Mexico and the Mexicans. To facilitate and make the work of his underlings at the Embassy more effective, he called them in to a cordial reunion and, after pleasantly giving them a few directives, ended the meeting thus: "Above all and before anything else, don't forget rule number four; that's the most important thing. Now let's go have us a whisky." And with a single gesture he made any commentary impossible.

His recommendation had a tremendous effect. Nobody could recall rule number four; in the offices everyone grew silent, thoughtful, depressed. High, middle, and low employees kept looking at each other trying to figure out from the expression on their faces if a companion remembered the famous rule. Things became desperate, and the most daring of them asked the head secretary (the one who told me the story) what rule number four was, for he didn't know it or perhaps had forgotten it, confessing to his ignorance little by little.

However, the head secretary couldn't remember the rule either. Everyone, up and down the scale, began inquiring but no one had the answer. So the one with the most guts, my friend, proposed the following: "Better than not complying with the order, let's propose a meeting with the chief, confessing our total ignorance, presenting any necessary excuses and accepting beforehand whatever sanctions he'll mete out. We must beg him to tell us what this number four rule is."

That was done, and when Mr. Morrow, with that marvelous sense of humor he possessed, went into a pretend fit while cordially repeating: "See? See? I do nothing but recommend a necessary and immensely important item for you to immediately infringe upon it, and what is worse, to continue doing it in my presence."

The look on the faces of the personnel was one of fear. They all had their eyes on the floor. An ominous silence pervaded the gathering. The immensely intelligent eyes of Mr. Morrow looked at all of them up and down, his fingers drumming impatiently on a work table, 'til finally my friend (today a very high dignitary in his country, then only a secretary at the third level) broke the silence and asked: "Boss, this situation is untenable; I am not the most qualified to ask so please excuse me; someone has to speak up and beg you to remind us what this rule is that we have shamelessly forgotten, or perhaps always ignored."

Mr. Morrow, feigning indignation, smacked the table so hard it shook up his assistants. Then he said, "Do you see? I told you; in this way nothing gets done. No wonder things are as they are! Rule number four, the key to our work is 'Let's not take ourselves too seriously.' Now that you know it, let's apply it. Let's not hear any more about it but have us a drink."

Anyway, when they tried to do something to help abstract art get rid of the revolutionary content in Mexican art, the daring friend I mentioned, holding a highly important position at the State Department in Washington, once again completely forgot all about rule number four. Due to this lamentable forgetfulness, there landed in Mexico our good man Filmer Stuart Cuckow Northrop, professor and philosopher with a book entitled *The Meeting of East and West* in which, by the way, he consigns to Mexico and us Mexicans a special role. He wisely includes José Clemente Orozco in that get-together of men between East and West plus in a special way, José Vasconcelos [at one time Minister of Education, —Trans.].

Since Mr. Northrop is a philosopher, and what's worse yet, a teacher of it, no one has figured out clearly what the sense or contents of his book are. Since he mentions me, the State Department figured that this professor would be of great importance to us Mexicans by lecturing us in a philosophy (which he, with charming good faith called "realist") consisting of affirming that Marxism was only good for the wastebasket. He repeated that at the National College, rigorously wearing a "smoking" suit while peeking at me from a corner of his eye with a smile that I could never decide whether it was due to his sense of irony or just simply a sudden stomach cramp.

It reminds me of that little ditty you mentioned once:

Bendigamos la pasta Ipana
para la sonrisa Panamericana.

(Let's bless Ipana toothpaste
for that Panamerican taste.)

The fact is that the only result obtained by that famous professor was the smile on the faces of all the members of the National College, including the most *'mochos'* (Catholic) among them. At least two had to cover their mouths to stifle their laughter because that night, precisely, the evening papers come out with the news that Mao Tse Tung's soldiers had reached the Indochinese frontier, taking eight billion people, in the most real of ways, through economics and arms, to that philosophical position that our speaker thought worthy of a paper basket.

After this event and through the newspapers and other solemn conferences, professor "Northern String" (as we literally can translate the name Northrop) concentrated on the issue that had brought him here: namely, art.

Before anything else, I must tell you that, not only Northrop, but the diplomacy from the North which controlled the strings, put into practice a strategy as well thought out as the Marshall Plan, for atomic plants and bomb warehouses that accidentally blow up periodically.

The philosopher arrived with great formality. The Department of Cultural Relations of our Secretary of Education presented him with a banquet with the assistance of the Secretary of Education and the First Secretary of the Embassy, since the *piece de resistance*, the ambassador, would come into action at the end, after his brilliant bishops, agile knights, and sturdy rooks had done the initial work. Upon his arrival, the professor had made his declaration to the press in accordance with a time when politics, strategy, and tactics based themselves on statements to the press as the most democratic procedure. In his declaration, Northrop asserted first that revolutionary art no longer has social or political content but is abstract, putting as an example the work of Georgia O'Keffe. Secondly, that Diego Rivera is not a revolutionary except for certain of his theories but that in his work he is a classicist. Third, that since abstract art is revolutionary, it is to be hoped that young Mexicans (since all Mexicans are revolutionaries) would become abstractionists.

Georgia O'Keffe is the wife of the most ingenious German photographer Stieglitz (since we know that the majority of North American artists are not born in the States, probably out of coquetry or elegance). O'Keffe's abstractions refer to paintings done in New Mexico and sometimes in New England. When she does abstractions in those places, she stylizes the curtains of a window for example, through which one perceives another one on the wall of an adobe house which doesn't make clear whether it's a granary or a chicken coop, nicely smooth and grey to make sure it is one hundred percent North American. Where abstraction happens in New Mexico, Georgia chooses skulls of mules or cattle that one finds in the desert plains where the animals die.

I suppose that professor "String of the North," or Northrop, sees these abstractions as realist or revolutionary since buzzards, worms, and the weather have "abstracted" the skin and flesh of the peeled skulls. But perhaps our realist professor refers to another kind of abstraction that might have impressed him more, if not by their content, by what they suggest. This happens when Georgia paints amplified flowers from eighty centimeters in diameter up to a meter, these flowers being intentionally chosen, orchids and cacti that open to the voluptuousness of any willing philosopher. I suppose that the reputation for being impetuous that we Mexicans have, forced Northrop to choose these kinds of abstractions to convince us.

The news from Mao Tse Tung arrived at the time of the anti-Marxist conference of our professor, and word from Paris where the masters of abstractionism, Picasso, and Braque, declared they had understood that their art was the result of bourgeois decadence and that as a result they were joining the French Communist Party, promising to create realistic paintings, taking as their general subject matter the lives of workers. They were re-editing our manifestoes of 1900, 1922, 1923, and 1924 without giving us credit but simply repeating our words of twenty-five years before, which that doesn't matter if they gain some good from it.

To finish up, I am sure that the accusation leveled at me of being a classicist, backed by the authority of an honest-to-god North American philosopher, had something to do with bringing 450,000 persons to my national exposition.

7

RIVERA IN ACTION

We formed the previous pages by putting together diverse but related parts. Left out was material that didn't fit those categories, so I am using them to form this chapter. It is interesting because his words strengthen Rivera's psychological and intellectual attributes.

His impressive culture, united to a fertile and always powerful imagination, allowed him to intervene in any discussion or subject of his time in such an original and skillful way that he knew how to blend exactitude with doubtful possibility, proven facts with chimeras, always submitting the rules of his thought to historic materialism, his leitmotiv.

Rivera was a scientist and a verifier of plastic forms, and also an ideologue. His ideas create possibilities and illuminate but do not verify. He was an artist in his reasoning as much as he was in his work.

I went to his fountain and filled my glass. Others have gone with sundry pails and done the same. The fountain of Rivera's words is located on a plain scorched by passion. His words are really thermal and sulphuric waters that can cure certain kinds of idealistic ailments, and can protect us from secular transcendentalism. I have spent a long time contemplating that landscape of vents which are his pronouncements, preferring it to the landscape of conferences and good behavior garbed in ashes. Here and there I have had to use pincers to pick up his incandescent words; now I contemplate them satisfied that they haven't lost heat or aggressiveness. Rivera can never be considered a dead volcano. We can look at his work as an eruption; at any moment he can tumble downhill, wrapped in his own lava, destroying any element that gets in the way of his eternity.

October 8, 1949. Perspective discovers aesthetic space in which, as Spengler puts it, "all things are submerged." It is that sense of profundity that in Wagner traverses forests and in Grünewald, master of somber greens, can cause tremors. For days I have thought about formulating a question for Rivera about perspective, but other themes have occupied his attention. Finally, today, I can ask: what terrain has modern painting gained in terms of perspective? This is his answer:

It is the custom to call perspective, *par excellence*, what is but one of them; in other words, what is monocular perspective employing a single point of escape. But this isn't more than a totally arbitrary convention derived from the spatial falsity of Euclidian geometry, which at first was a correct and valuable means of easily translating a sketch or architectonic project to the measurable terrain of its execution. That has nothing to do with the spatial reality of the physical world since, being but a medium at the service of human beings, it is totally false in the field of physical, psychological and mathematical reality, since mankind is not made up entirely of cross-eyed people who are, at the same time, complete paralytics totally lacking in tactile sensibility.

It happened precisely at the start of the decay of the Renaissance when this convention for the purely technical use of architects was given the category of a dictatorial norm for the representative values of the physical world in painting. It isn't true and, to convince ourselves of this, it is enough to look at the painting of epochs prior to the Renaissance. In no part of this world was such a conventional degeneration accepted, not even in the most fortunate epoch of Greek decadence, to which the Renaissance artists attributed the invention of their own creature, as well as its adoption.

In reality, even in the weakest Greek paintings you will find at least a plurality of points of escape, corresponding as much to the principal key points of view, if we are dealing with mural painting, or to the different centers of interest in a composition if the work is the product of an easel.

Already during the Renaissance, Paolo Uccello fought heroically against this ridiculous convention meant for cross-eyed and insensible paralytics, substituting it with a spatial construct of volumes, more logical and much more dynamic and plastic. Uccello tended towards a more realistic perspective, in other words, a spherical one. From that we get the legend that he went crazy after drawing so many rose windows. It's possible that some document might be extant, possibly in the memory of his contemporaries, about the master's pursuits since, truly, the geometric sketch of a true (spherical) perspective of space could be called a rose window by those who don't understand the mathematical nature of what they are seeing. Uccello's search remains a mysterious conjecture; it came after the discovery of the marvelous works of his that remain since, in these, it is only possible to sense the effort he made towards a real spherical perspective.

Centuries had to pass 'til a Mexican, who by doing it should be considered a great man, presented a clear, fixed mathematical form to its true spherical content, something we painters sensible to space have been fighting for since Mathias Grünewald and Titian to this day. I refer to the spherical perspective established on an absolutely scientific basis by master Enrique A. Serrano. He is the author of the first treatise of spherical perspective, and the inventor, besides, of the apparatus necessary to verify and experimentally adjust its mathematical proportions. These apparatus have been stolen (with no credit given) and utilized by scientific and industrial pirates for the fabrication of cameras with wide-angle lenses capable of photographing the entire existing space above that ground when placed on it.

The discovery and, better said, the scientific construction of spherical perspective by Serrano, is unquestionably the most important acquisition made by the art sciences since the Renaissance to this day and constitute a true glory for Mexico. It is also a terrible and inexplicable shame for this same Mexico not only to have underestimated and practically ignored the great man, that 'perspectographer' whose conquest is a diamond of inestimable value in the jewel box Mexican mural painting, built to enrich and embellish mankind.

November 6, 1949. Regarding those artists that begin their careers full of self-confidence but lament the social medium and the lack of opportunities to realize their work, Rivera told me:

When we began, we had no opportunities; we prepared in silence and created our own opportunity.

Regarding the world of painters already formed, with sufficient work to be considered young masters, Rivera spoke in the following way:

It seems to me that each of them has considerable intrinsic value and that they are called upon to determine this plastic Mexican phenomenon. The work they have already realized has a positive value. Among them we must mention women such as Isabel Villaseñor, Olga Costa, Aurora Reyes and Frida Kahlo. This last has given modern Mexican painting a note, in my estimation, that is the most pure, profound and genuinely popular Mexican thing available. Other painters have done excellent mural and studio work: men such as Jesús Guerrero Galvan, Raúl Angiano, Leopoldo Méndez, Paul O'Higgins, and above all, Juan O'Gorman, since if one had to choose ten important works of the last ten years representing the muralist movement, we'd have to include among them O'Gorman's magnificent mural at the *Pátzcuaro* library, something that will be mentioned in art history as one of the most valuable works of our muralist tradition.

But these are not the only painters who have done murals: Alfredo Zalce is not just a possibility but a magnificent reality. He has painted very beautiful pieces. Besides these well-formed artists, there is one who, due to his age and time spent at work, besides its quality and volume, is among the top and should be placed in the first rank in his own right: Javier Guerrero. And for very diverse reasons and by an analogy of values in his own field, volume and capacity, there is someone else worthy of being distinguished. His name is Manuel Rodríguez Lozano.

Contrasting with these valuable names, there is a group of three quite young artists, extremely young, who have demonstrated great worth, not just in their attempts but in a joint work whose quality, observation, plasticity, social content and disinterested attitude is such that it is a pity Mexican critics have ignored them. I am referring to the mural executed in the humble building of the Washerwomen's Cooperative entitled "Unwed

Mothers" in *Coyoacan.* It is a work of socialist realism so good it brought tears of emotion to the female workers, tears that art critics are incapable of shedding for a painting because they reserve them for their monetary successes. I am talking about the work that painters Monroy, Bustos and Estrada did, all of them with names famous in Mexican painting of the 19th century, and that now will pass into the 20th. A talented woman collaborated with them, coming from quite far to become Mexican: Fany Rabinovich. All four were disciples of Frida Kahlo.

The possibility that the muralist movement will continue isn't something to be doubted but verified. In the three generations of painters following Orozco, Siqueiros and Rivera, plus two men of the same generation, there is all that is required. What we need is to give them work and this depends on the State and private initiative. New painters have the responsibility of its continuance, if there is a field of play, or its decay for lack of it. We have capable artists with more than enough talent. The only thing needed is civic consciousness and an interest in the development of native art not only from official organisms but from private sources because mural painting should not be converted, for whatever reason, into a pension depending on the largesse of the State. It should come from the people and be for the people. The people should underwrite it, be it done in grocery stores and greasy spoons or residences and palaces. If mural painting is once again created in such places, as happened in the past, it will be an affirmation that Mexico has began to experience a national life and is headed towards real independence, meaning both economic and cultural.

February 12, 1950. I contact Rivera to continue our talks. The artist arrives and chooses the warmth of a Chinese tea served in fine Oaxacan crockery. He is exhausted, having worked continuously from nine in the morning to six in the evening by the time I arrived at his studio. Besides, he was upset, being unable to obtain in time the customs permits for a painting meant to go with its purchasers to the States the next morning. The painting is nearly finished. It's a portrait of a fine woman, soft, exquisite. Rivera chose for her a shawl from his collection, bougainvillea in color, that harmonized with the color of her skin. From his palette there surfaced a distant smile, full of loving sphinxes. He had almost finished it in nine hours, with his eyes badly irritated, full of tears.

He has worked quite hard these last few months, doing portraits whose spontaneous or required models show up and disappear constantly from his workspace. We have seen the gestation, birth and plenitude of many of them, and observed the way he resolves the problems of the face, the slow foreshortening of the hands, the great and absolute pleasure of the master before the mysterious vibrations of human expression. His genius begins to enter a face the way the humblest Indians enter a market, from all sides of a plaza, the way soldiers will lay siege to a fortress, circling it, their lances extended, or how night descends over a village. This pictorial militancy, let's call it that, affects the entire painting, which is realized perfectly by the surrounding harmonies, leaping from an eyebrow to a hand, from a fold in the skirt to the undulation of a curl, leaving, at the end of the workday, small white ovals, like the clearing in a moody forest, or like voluntary pools that he will fill with shadows the next day. Magic pulse and equilibrium, circular movement of color, obedience of parts to the whole, which Rivera repeats day after day, week after week, in one of the most impressive aesthetic exercises of our time!

March 12, 1950. Mr. Chaman Lal, a Hindu poet and sociologist, came to Diego Rivera's studio dressed in the unmistakably oriental style: pants called jodphurs, a tight waist coat, cap like Nehru's and a pastor's neck line. Mr. Lal carried with him a book entitled Hindu America, of which he is the author and in which he proposes that from the most ancient of times, the American continent and its inhabitants were known by adventurous Hindu colonizers, merchants, architects and priests, and that Mexico and Central America, undoubtedly the cradle of the New World civilization, show innumerable signs and ruins of the culture and religious philosophy current in India.

What a precious honey bee for Rivera's sensibility! The master abandoned for a moment the portrait of Columba Dominguez he was working on and chatted with the distinguished intellectual from New Delhi. The two got involved in a conversation full of belly buttons and parasols. I have no idea what they talked about, having arrived late to this conference of tea and prickly pear. But Rivera, impressed by the visit of this Hindu, gave way to his scientific imagination:

Mr. Chaman Lal's book, destined to prove the deep similitude of our culture with India's is, besides that, interesting and authentic. I adhere to his ideas. Humanity was born around the ocean called today the Arctic Glacial Ocean, simultaneously for all human groups, and developed there for hundreds of thousands of years when the ocean was like a vast and marvelous semi-tropical lake and the Antarctic continent observed similar conditions. During that time, the terrestrial ring hanging between the Tropics of Cancer and Capricorn, on either side of the equator, was a zone positively torrid. The life of man and his contemporary vertebrates was totally impossible within it. Later on, when the poles began to cool, humans began to spread towards the tropics and the Equator through all paths available till northerners mixed with southerners.

Both nuclei, that from the north composed of people we today call Mongoloid, and that from the south exclusively containing the human type we today call Negroid, when they mixed, produced all the ethnic shades of what is called, for political convenience, the Arian or white race.

This is not a new theory, but the logical conclusion derived from the findings and investigations of Soviet men of science, who have found thousands of vegetal, animal and human fossils, identical to the species and families we find today in our tropical latitudes of the northern hemisphere, with some inroads south. In the Antarctic region they found fossils identical to beings inhabiting the African inter-tropic, with shoots towards the north.

At the same time, Soviet scientists have learned that marriages between Mongoloids and Negroids that could be considered pure, result, after several generations beginning with the seventh, perfect Arian types (stupendous platinum blond females with facial angles of 90 degrees and blue eyes), available to any Count de Gobineau who insists on the superiority of the white race. True proof of this is the brilliant end of the Gustav Adolf Swedish monarchy, or the recent reign of the "Fuhrer," who fell before the forces of Mongoloid Russians.

Without doubt we find Mongoloids from Alaska to the tip of Patagonia, Negroids even in Monte Albán, Oaxaca, and on the horizon of the "La Venta" culture, using the language of archeologists and accepting proofs marvelously sculpted in the language of artists. This also avoids difficulties of interpretation about the heads of elephants in *Copán* and the bodies buried in Monte Albán, just as it explains the unity of successive American cultures beginning with the archaic and those that have similarities with Eurasia and North Africa.

So we know why the figurine from *Tlatilco* resembles those from China, from Mesopotania, and archaic Mediterranean figures.

This is the similarity what Gandhi called "amazing" between certain periods of American art and contemporary ones from India, and the architectural identity of the plane, in its form and function, between ancient Peking and ancient Teotihuacan, etc.

All of this must be seen without the need to think, as some persons as myopic as they are idiotic imagine that Mexico is a retarded Egypt or Egypt an advanced Mexico, when, in reality, they are contemporaneous since they proceed from cultures that have the same origin: Mongoloid in the north and Negroid in the south, with equal mixtures in each case, due to the crossing of the tropics.

All this is clear and simple, but it isn't accepted yet in any roundtable or congress of "occidentalized" learned men (because they find themselves in the full sunset of their fame and culture). And why, you might ask, isn't it accepted? Because culture today has interrupted its march thanks to a paper curtain, paper printed in dollar bills, which even turn prudent mathematicians who avoid upsetting governments that pay their wages. They can't accept discoveries coming from inside the terrifying iron curtain, whether it be evident proof of the origin and routes of mankind (Anglo-Saxons are white and must be purity incarnate), or clear and simple proof of airplanes with new types of motors, reducing super bombers that carry atomic bombs to the level of mechanical toys; those bombs that only frighten Secretaries of War, who go mad and run into the street in their pajamas shouting, "Save yourselves! The Russians are falling on top of us!"

April 9, 1950. I find Rivera seated in a leather couch in the company of the artist Rodolfo Galván discussing the scenography for the next work for theater by the novelist José Revueltas.

The master, like a kid with a new toy, has gotten excited with the work and is discussing set designs with a small reproduction of the theater in front of him. Two mobile platforms are involved. The right side sticks out of the stage and represents a Chinese restaurant, The Shanghai, where morphine addicts chat. Rivera took as his model a nearby grocery store that exhibits the Virgin of Solitude in a high niche. The set on the left represents a neighborhood hotel, above which are the balconies of room number seven, with railings. The style of the hotel is clearly one of poor urban taste an symbolizes, as Rivera says, "those knife thrusts that capitalism delivers to the architecture of the old city." The background is taken up by a large church, with its quadrant of sun gone today, in such a way that the spectator will see one of those typical local corners of the Mexican capital.

Rivera started to reminisce, turning memories into presences and evocations into ironies:

The Church of La Soledad and Santa Cruz has been the cathedral of the picaresque world. Professional thieves and prostitutes established their bank there, so it was disinfected and closed down during the Revolution. It had a wealth of *retablos* of which some, the best, ended up in the museum, but other very interesting ones went to certain private collections, especially those of painters. Today, when the curve of the Revolution has bent down softly towards a bourgeois consolidation, bringing with it its highly important industrialization and full tolerance of the Catholic religion, today that old church we have been talking about has returned to its old glory. The sacristy is being restored, no expense barred, a magnificent example of *Tolsiana* architecture. It has been rediscovered drowning in miserable repairs. The plaza has gone back to its original dimensions, tearing down an entire block that had invaded it at the time of the Reform, when it was considered an empty field and sold to foreigners; to Spaniards, Frenchmen, and some Germans, who erected neighborhoods similar to our apartment complexes.

It was precisely thanks to them that the neighborhood, possessing an extraordinarily sinister beauty and a tremendous architectonic value, has received terrible modernist knife thrusts thanks to urban planning executed by personages that must indubitably be devout followers of La Soledad and of the Santa Cruz.

The same historical logic presides over the transformation of the entire neighborhood of la Soledad, so immensely interesting and fascinating from a plastic, social and literary point of view. They have established a huge truck center there since the promoters of that industry did away with the ancient mule stables that dominated the area, which in the old days was influential in the presidential assumption of power. All this has occurred thanks to the modernist taste of those who secretly want to bring back their old devotion to La Soledad and the Santa Cruz. This demonstrates that no matter how many Semitic-Hispanic and other knife thrusts of a foreign nature Mexico receives in complicity with those abominable modernist pseudo-architects, the country will conserve intact its core traditional sense, especially its negative modes.

Let me explain this matter of negative modes: in the past, among crumbling scenery and gorgeous architecture, we could find hidden corners where we sang, seated in a circle around a live iguana, while marihuana went around:

Hey, hey, hey, what a crazy iguana,
look, look, how it opens its mouth,

because the beastie took an active role in the ritual and, looking for the magic smoke like the participants, received it in its darling little snout as it emerged from our filthy snouts singing:

This grass is from the country
of old tools, harvested in Tepic,
refined with so much alcohol
that it makes my ears
buzz, buzz, buzz…

But now, "*doña Juanita,*" harvested in mass and grown even in Grand Central park in New York by Mexicans who enjoy a joke, has our neighborhood of La Soledad lacking in the guitars and "the extraordinary" that don Ramón María del Valle Inclán liked so much:

It passed by here, by here it passed.
that marihuana of our consolation…

The Soledad has established in every nook the terrifying mademoiselle Morphine, so that we can be at the level of the Hispanic-Jewish-Syrian-Lebanese dealers and of the shining trucks that reach Guatemala, Nautla, Oaxaca, and the like, to the blessings of Laredos, all of Texas, Juárez and neighboring locations. This marvelous substance has produced its first literary fruit in this work of José Revueltas that I find marvelous. That is why I am working on its scenography with Rodolfo Galván.

All its personages, marvelously defined, are morphine dealers or just amateurs, except for a poor student who thought he was for the working man and who, in order to save a beautiful morphine addict in the depths of a Chinese coffee house, sells out the workers of a general strike of transportation. The Chinese owner of the joint frustrates the student's attempt to save the girl. The young man was a victim of the girl's lover and of the director of a professional college who thought he was the girl's father as revealed by a magnificent old prostitute, the central figure in the work. All of them, even a blind metal worker, guided by a pensioner from the correctional school, are morphine dealers. Revueltas achieves a frightening climax having the student die hung above the fleshy white lily of a toilet. The police and the Order of Columbus members plus the entire morphine underworld in the pay of the transportation company, want to break the strike and blow up the gas tanks for the truck line, attributing the crime to the strike leaders as a pretext to have them thrown in jail as incendiaries and murderers.

The plot is a complete view of all the parasitical social classes allied against field and urban workers.

April 16, 1950. Young painters are upset that they weren't invited to the Venice Biennial and made declarations in the newspapers. I asked Rivera about it and this is the answer he gave me:

There is no worse wedge than one from the same tree, nor must we forget that a brave bitch bites its masters. It's not new for Mexican painters to protest and attack other Mexican painters. I have heard that those of the second generation, those who, a few years ago were very young, have stated that they want nothing to do with the so-called "three great ones," of Mexican painting, Orozco, Siqueiros and me. Nothing would be more worthy of celebration if that were the truth, for it would mean that such protesters were talented, but unfortunately, that is not the case.

I should tell you that in that second generation there are some I consider great Mexican artists and who are, as I have mentioned to you on several occasions, Frida Kahlo, the purest and most deeply Mexican while being extremely modern in her manner. There is Juan O'Gorman who, in his easel work, has many connections with Frida and who, with the sincerity of a great artist dedicated his murals at the airport at Balbuena to her. There is also Alfredo Zalce, a truly great painter, and Pablo O'Higgins who is in no hurry or impatient to gain international recognition, sure as he must be that his magnificent work will someday resonate at an international level.

But that protest is absolutely ridiculous. The Venice exposition every two years invites some thirty painters of salient personality, recognized at an international level. Each gets his turn and only a worldwide reputation makes opportunity available.

When the Venice Biennial did a show of Renoir, what great master would have dared to protest for his own glorification? They felt proud to see in it a triumph for the school of Paris, that's all.

When years later, as an extremely exceptional homage (since it's customary to invite just one painter of each nationality) they invited Pablo Picasso, Georges Braque, Henri Matisse and André Derain, nobody was bothered nor thought of protesting, not even the great master León Bonnat nor the extremely well known Raúl Duffy because everyone knew that Matisse was the deacon and head of the list that included Bonnard, Duffy, Deraín and others. They knew Picasso to be the first initiator of the cubist tendency and Deraín of organized naturalism. The designation was taken as a glory of the Parisian school, and any painter form there would have been ashamed to feel discontent with an invitation addressed to the deans of his school; and we must take into account that there were personalities who, with the exception of Picasso and Matisse, could just as well have substituted for those invited.

But they have common sense over there, and *esprit de corp*, something that we frequently lack around here, though we bear plenty of fickle passions, like feeling sadness over the good fortune of others.

For the same reason that Venice invited Picasso, Matisse, Braque and Deraín as homage to the Parisian school, now they have invited Orozco, Siqueiros, Tamayo and your servant as representatives of what the world understands to be the Mexican school, and as an homage to it. Those who protest, saying they have nothing to do with us, are correct. We are painters of the Mexican school and they belong to the international family that paints while looking at foreign magazines of art. That is why neither Venice nor any other place has reason to invite them.

The protest was a sterile one.

They simply expose themselves to receive a reply exactly as the painter Caprotti de Monza, representing Venice, told me he gave to someone that was accusing him of having made the selection without knowing Mexican painting well, and this was his reply: "You are wrong in your appreciation. The Venice committee and I know Mexican art perfectly well, and it is precisely because of that that we have invited those we have invited and not you. Perhaps in a few years your personality will have perfected itself sufficiently and your fame will have grown enough for us to do it. Be patient and work."

May 21, 1950. Rivera has been drawing on the walls of the National Palace with unbelievable ferocity, twenty and twenty-two hours a day! On Thursday of the week before he started to paint at seven a.m. and didn't finish until nine a.m. the next morning, allowing for a seven-hour break in order to return to the charge that night and part of Saturday's dawn. One could call it gigantomania at the service of contemporary art.

His only assistant is a raw youth whom the master calls El Yuca because the boy comes from Yucatan. This boy carries and hands him his horizon line, the level, the square and the brushes. He has everything in order and doesn't allow anyone to go up the improvised ladder. On a day when Rivera was absent, the Treasury Secretary, Mr. Ramón Beteta tried to climb up to observe personally the development of the painting, and a voice shouted, "Hey, you! Get down from there! It's forbidden to fool around up there!" It was Yuca, Rivera's small watchdog. The Secretary didn't know what to say, and at that moment the painter showed up, frightening poor Yuca.

On the first floor of the Palace's patio, to the left of the staircase, Rivera paints the fourth fresco of a series we could call, "the Labor and the Days. "The first one represents the ancient Tenochtitlan market place; the second one all the uses of color (dry cleaners, the painting of codices, the decoration of buildings, and the cultivation of cotton as well as the extraction of rubber, plus hunting, fishing, the making of carbon and the exploitation of forests). The third one shows the art of feathers and gold, with the extraction of auriferous sands, the hunt of birds of rich plumage, and the various arts of transformation.

The fourth is an extraordinary fresco by Rivera, representing the huge festival of the goddess Chicomecóatl that took place in Papantla with the help of surrounding villages. Chicomecóatl (seven snakes) was called by the Indians "the mother of the gods," "the heart of the earth," and "our grandmother." A pre-Hispanic Ceres, Mother of Maintenance. According to Father Sahagún, they painted her with a crown on her head. In her right hand she held a vase, and in her left a round shield with a flower. She was the first woman who began to make food.

In the midst of a blinding chromaticism, which condenses and expands the energies of the tropics, appears the pyramid of Tajín (wooded hill), the game of the Flyers, and a procession of bearers of offerings to *Chicomecóatl.* High up, the clumps of houses in the mist of greenery; below, Mexicans come to trade products with the natives, carrying the great *Yacatecutli,* god of merchants (the Latin Mercury) with his *xtatl* (walking stick) and the sacred *acayietl* (censer) while a warrior is giving secret instructions to a *tlacuilo* (painter or scribe, maker of hieroglyphics) dealing with the defense of that dominium that soon would fall to the Aztecs. Poetry, with its cornucopia of offerings, and politics, with its spy dressed as a merchant, meet here in this pre-Hispanic image so full of moving, dazzling rituals.

Number seven, so vital in the oldest symbologies, appears in the number of the temple steps, in every niche, floor and allegorical adornment. Regarding the Game of the Flyer, that marionette of air still seen in some towns in the south of the Veracruz area, which draws exclamations of wonder from national and foreign tourists, we should say that it has an astronomical origin, representing the four solar movements, whose rays descend slowly down to earth; the reference is to the four equinoxes, when the Game was performed during the equinox feasts.

Those, in large strokes, are the lineaments of this Rivera fresco, one of the most beautiful in the National Palace.

If to the artistic emotion, the poetry of its description, we add its historical fidelity, we have an extremely valuable representation of our racial genius. Rivera paints remembering things, not inventing them. Just the Tenochtitlán fresco took him a year and a half to document, investigating, checking the annals of the past, so that the painter is also a pedagogue who conveys his findings in a monumental way.

The fifth fresco Rivera will undertake will deal with the extraction of rubber, chewing gum, asphalt, and the cultivation of vanilla and tobacco.

The sixth will deal with the arrival of European products.

The seventh will have to do with mining, cattle, and the cultivation of wheat.

Then will come the colonial market with its fundamental characteristics, followed by themes of Mexico in the 19th century, embracing the Church and the Reform. He will include the Porfirio Díaz period and, lastly, the Revolution with the changes in the methods of cultivation, the mechanization of the land and the growth of industry. To end, there will be a contrast to the ancient Tenochtitlán: the Tenochtitlán of the future.

All this will be done in two years of work. More than 300 square meters of wall will be painted at 500 pesos per square meter and a total cost of nearly 135,000 pesos "since mural painting," the artist confessed, "is an economic disaster for Mexican painters even after the better tariffs obtained through presidential accord and the integration of a national commission for mural painting."

There is the notion that Rivera might undertake the second floor of the National Palace, but the contract has not been signed.

We have called this series, "The Labor and the Days." Rivera names it "History of the Methods of Exchange and Production." The conception is of a huge ring whose diamond is the epic poem of the central stairway, where its profusely elaborated fitting spills its gold claws in a succession of thematic shafts. It's a ring for a giant, which Mexico will wear on its middle finger and will flaunt with pride in all the great festivities of the nation.

Looking at these frescos by Rivera, we recall the old epigram of Jeremiah that appears in front of the General History of the Things of New Spain and which reads: I shall bring unto you a nation from beyond, robust and ancient; a nation whose language thou shall not understand… It will attack your cornfields and devour your sons and daughters."

Something Spain did not understand right away.

June 18, 1950. For a few days now it has been known in Mexico that one of the prizes of the Venice Biennale was awarded to the painter David Siqueiros. Nothing better than to seek Rivera's opinion about this Mexican triumph. Here is what he told me:

I have had direct news about how things went, sent by Italians that I know. Such information coincides with what my friend Jorge Juan Crespo de la Serna, Vice-President of the International Association of Art Critics, has told me. With those antecedents, let me say the following:

Their best painters and critics went to Venice to battle for purist art. The order given by the Association just mentioned was to act with a wide sense of criteria and justice, and at the same time in defense of pure and independent art, which is what the syndicate of the *marchants de tableaux et d'objets d'art* does business by.

There was a consignment from Paris of the four great cubists (Pablo Picasso, Georges Braque, Juan Gris and André Léger) corresponding to a consignment from the four great Mexicans. Besides that, they had a great show of the old master Matisse, the last survivor of the great painters of his generation; another one of Gino Severini, the Italian comrade that went from Futurist to being companion to Picasso's group. There were strong paintings from Belgium and Holland, and attempts by good North Americans plus some disciples of Siqueiros. Spain sent as reinforcement an entire room of the enormous don Francisco de Goya y Lucientes and another of the great painter José Gutiérrez Solana, dead a while back.

Nevertheless, from the time the dangerous boxes containing Mexican paintings were opened, the professional curiosity of critics and painters leaped onto them, producing a veritable sensation because they had to bow before the quality of form and content of our work and the force it represented. When the exposition was opened to the public—and this is the most important thing—the Venetian public, the artistic public, didn't have a doubt and chose the Mexican section as its favorite.

A Venetian citizen has written me. Look what he tells me: "I address this letter to you with the emotion of having seen and heard with my own eyes and ears my Venetian compatriots, gathered above the Rialto and the whole length of the Grand Canal and its San Marcos plaza, there to discuss the paintings of you folks and to exclaim, *Il Orozco e il Tintoretto del Messico, e il Rivera e quello qui a fatto la cappella Sixtina dell'America*." And he adds, "This was how Venetians behaved, as tradition has it, during the time of our great painting."

That color-loving people were attracted by the color of my work, Orozco's genial perspective, Tamayo's palette, and the chiaroscuro emotivity of Siqueiros.

When the moment for the jury to act arrived, (and we know that there isn't a jury of aesthetics free from pre-conceptions and last minute arrangements), the moment had also arrived to define 'pure and independent art.' There were various scrutinies, and even though everyone kept affirming that the Mexican exhibit was the most important in the exposition, there was no majority to give it the prize on the first count. In this count only two Mexicans got a vote. A number of art purists voted for Tamayo and a certain number of new realists went for me. They stated that Orozco, having died, belonged in the category of the retrospectives. Others voted for Picasso, others for Matisse, the representative from Holland voted for the Dutch painter, the one from Belgium for the Belgian painter Constantino Permeke. Conditions were such that it might prove impossible to award a first prize. Diplomacy began to play its part... You may not know this but Mexican representatives and art critics are quite good diplomats; sometimes our wives are even better.

After more scrutiny, they arrived at the following conclusions: First: among the votes given for the first prize, Matisse had more than any other. Matisse could be considered the last great painter of the post-impressionist Parisian school; he had really been my teacher. The same could be said of Tamayo as all evidence showed, and of the young Picasso as well. Secondly: They weren't going to reach any agreement about us nor was it considered possible to give anyone the second prize since to offer it to Picasso or to Matisse would have been the most ridiculous thing the jury could have done. That's where diplomacy took over. With Orozco dead, and no accord possible for Tamayo and me since the purists and the neo-realists were at odds, there emerged a brilliant and magnificent salvation: Siqueiros' emotion and new technique, whose worth everyone recognized. There were in him, in part, neo-realistic elements of great force, and also abstract elements obvious to the purists. The proposed solution was adopted by acclamation, so the prize was given to Siqueiros, for there were no immediate challengers to the four great Frenchmen, nor to the post-cubist-Braquean-matissist Tamayo. Besides... eliminated was public enemy number one, the first *insurgé mexicain de l'affaire Rivera,* the same one who around 1918 fought against purist art by defending a neo-realistic art with a social content for the masses. In that way we had unity: the ones for Tamayo and Rivera in the person of Siqueiros, who received twelve votes for the first prize, the scrutinizers admitting they had voted for Matisse. In the next to the final scrutiny, unanimously, they gave Siqueiros the second prize of the Mexican section.

It was magnificent that Siqueiros should triumph because he deserved moneys given the Biennal by the museum of the Brazilian city of Sao Pablo. In that very same museum, public opinion and by order of the mayor, a show of the excellent and famous Brazilian painter Cándido Portinari (follower, first of Rivera and then Picasso, with some elements of Siqueiros) was shut down because this great artist was a Communist. He was also a senator kicked out of Parliament by the police of Mr. Eurico Gaspar Dutra who, by the way, did a bad job judging the painting of his famous compatriot, saying that his paintings were crap. Thus, for a Mexican painter who is an active member of our Communist Party to have received moneys from the museum of Sao Pablo was a resounding smack on the face of Mr. Dutra.

To wrap this up: the prize given David has great importance from several points of view. Undoubtedly, among the group of paintings sent to the Biennale, the ones by Siqueiros, besides their plastic force, had the greatest political content and major incisive power as painting of revolt and propaganda against war. Also, his paintings were closer in style and feel to his murals than, say, mine. The jury, however constituted (and juries for expositions are the same anywhere), was obligated, by the same force that Mexican mural painting has acquired in today's marketplace, to admit its superiority precisely because it contained a shared social and political content regardless of differences, tendencies and temperament.

The actual movement initiated in Paris 25 years after we began it in Mexico and the USSR, with some token actions in the United States, must have had great influence in this matter.

Anyway, it is an important victory against purist art precisely where up to now it had been a sacred cow. Obviously, the spectacle of cities destroyed, of the pain, hunger and terror felt by civil masses during the war, has prepared an environment in which the masses were interested in their own interests forcefully and with exaltation.

The danger of war hangs over that which survived death. No people want war, only the merchants of armaments and explosives, drinkers of blood, mechanized vampires and assassins of nearly a million women, children and old people in Japan. They are the only ones who want a new massacre in order to accumulate millions and millions of dollars, gathering natural products, finished products and work as payment for theoretical millions in paper money backed by the strength of the imperialist police active as civilian constabularies, air, marine and land armies.

That is why the echo of tears in David's sigh (who never lacked the adequate sentimental accent perfect to reach the masses when they hurt), has shamed the aesthetes, managers of the money made from the blood of assassinated peoples, to the point where they have had to fold their hands and render homage to that painting hand which whacks the snouts of the accomplices of the high bourgeoisie.

That is why we who belong to and are on the same barricade with David's triumph of tears and sighs should be delighted.

Let's leave the aesthetes to bite their nails and think how 'tears and sigh' would make an excellent title for the sentimental music of any author disdained by the great makers of symphonies. Let's leave them thoughtful... surely with a bit of fear while the struggle for peace continues magnificently in spite of the necrophagous police who want war disguised as a *pax romana*.

They have begun to understand that we will win the peace because we *are* all the peoples of the earth. Besides, half of humanity has the better armies to back up the true desire for peace felt by women and men in the world.

Those who need to fatten their ideas with the blood of people opposed to death know, even though they keep it quiet and pretend the opposite, that if in spite of the universal desire for peace within the only true democracy, which is socialism, they insist and ignite war again, it will happen with absolute mathematical certainty that they will be defeated within weeks, months or years.

It is necessary that the Mexican masses, including all social classes that don't want a new universal killing spree, celebrate in a great public act the triumph of Mexican painting in the person of David Alfaro Siqueiros, by offering him an extraordinary popular welcome. By that act we would show that we are not dealing with a manifestation of a provincial inferiority complex praised by European approval, but an affirmation of our strength facing the present historical reality. Confronted with such palpable evidence, they will have had to say yes, those who would have said no. It's also necessary to note that if our bourgeoisie and petty bourgeoisie have existed smelling Europe's behind and shaking their tail imitating their style with twenty-five years of delay, now the vital part of Europe gets in tune with what we the artists of the

Mexican people created twenty-five years ago. We are equal and can share an embrace.

June 25, 1950. Rivera has pulled out of his waistcoat a few papers and shows them to me. The first one has been his since the 21st of March and is a cable from Berlin signed by Arnold Sweig which, in the name of the German Academy of the Arts, congratulates with the greatest cordiality the Mexican Mr. Diego Rivera, for having been chosen as an active member of that corporation.

The artist doesn't make any comment, just continues working.

Afterwards I read a letter from Italy, signed by Gisela Figuerola Demaria. (What must Gisela be like? She must be thin, with Mediterranean eyes. Gisela has never been to Mexico and doesn't know how Diego Rivera is.) In the letter she says that she has just graduated from the Academy of Bellas Artes in Brera, Milan, as professor of art history and that the thesis she presented was a study of the Mexican colossus, Diego Rivera. It was well liked and she has been invited to amplify it and publish it in one of the editions of the Scheiwiller House.

Lastly, and because of its anecdotal value, I am transcribing the letter which, on the 12th of June, Mr. Fernando Gamboa, the official representative from Mexico at the huge exposition taking place in the home of the Renaissance, sent to Rivera:

"My admired and dear Diego:

"Mexican art has gained a decisive battle in its first presentation in Europe. The work of the four Mexican painters shown at the Biennial has been such an extraordinary revelation for artists, the large public, the critics and directors of this country and all Europe, that the Mexican pavilion has been declared the most important, vigorous, and original of those presented this year. The names of Diego Rivera, Orozco, Siqueiros and Tamayo resound constantly everywhere. Your name was already known and was famous in these latitudes, but today, in front of your art, all recognize in Rivera one of the greatest artists of our time.

"When the public enters the exposition gardens, they make a special trip to our pavilion, bypassing the 21 from other countries and the 60 rooms of Italy's pavilion. This is how quick and brilliant has been Mexico's prestige. A new world has opened up for many, a world of independent thought, of force and passion, of monumental conception, of epic poetry. Anyway, the magnificent voice of Mexican painters is resounding with a marvelous renaissance strength, and everyone hears it with their heads full of new ideals.

"That the first prize has been given to Matisse is proof that the interests created around the so-called 'free' art continue being powerful. The fact that Siqueiros got the second international prize demonstrates that realism, such as it is practiced in Mexican art, can't be ignored and must be recognized as one of the essential seeds in contemporary plastic art. How stunning will be the victory of your painting, of Mexican painting, that one of the most distinguished European critics has publicly declared that the frescos at *Chapingo* are 'the Sistine Chapel of the Mexican Revolution!'

"And how much we will have to say about Mexican painting! I only want to tell you that after having seen the Sistine, Giotto and so much else, Susana and I have cried with the purest emotion: "How great is Diego Rivera! How formidable is Mexican muralism!

"We will see you soon and talk at length. Our most enthusiastic felicitations for the success your art is finding, and for the huge success of Mexican art. Long live Mexico! A warm embrace from me and Susana for you and Frida, sent to you with respect and unchanging affection. Fernando Gamboa."

July 30, 1950. This is my last interview with the master. (I still published another article dated August 8 but as a wrap-up of all the work.) It was a bright Sunday and Rivera was bubbling with good humor. Lola Alvarez Bravo, there with us, took a photograph of the two of us to perpetuate the memory. I was feeling badly knowing I was going to lose him. Not that he was going to disappear physically (he had seven more years of life and work ahead of him) but because, once my task was done, it would be quite difficult to see him as often as I had.

Rivera, seeing me with my pencil ready, smiled and said:

I must say goodbye with this one, my dear poet and friend Cardona Peña, goodbye also to *El Nacional* which gave us such hospitality. Goodbye also to your readers who, with exemplary patience, have read more than fifty articles written by you on my life and work. Thanks and greetings from Diego Rivera.

Now that the true eternity of the artist has begun, I visit my papers to gather the passionate gold of his utterances. This isn't a complete nor a calculated book, but a moment, a fugacity stolen from oblivion. But I think that, with its limitations and hurried pressure, it enriches the bibliography of the painter and helps the work of analysis and thought which will undoubtedly come in the future. I am not made to write biographies and histories, but to celebrate the word of creative spirits and be an impressionist of the moment.

Here is my version of Diego Rivera, the one I gathered from his lips. How? According to Goethe's beautiful explanation, "following the impression of the moment, without thinking of an artistic plan, the way one spills water from a jar."

• • •

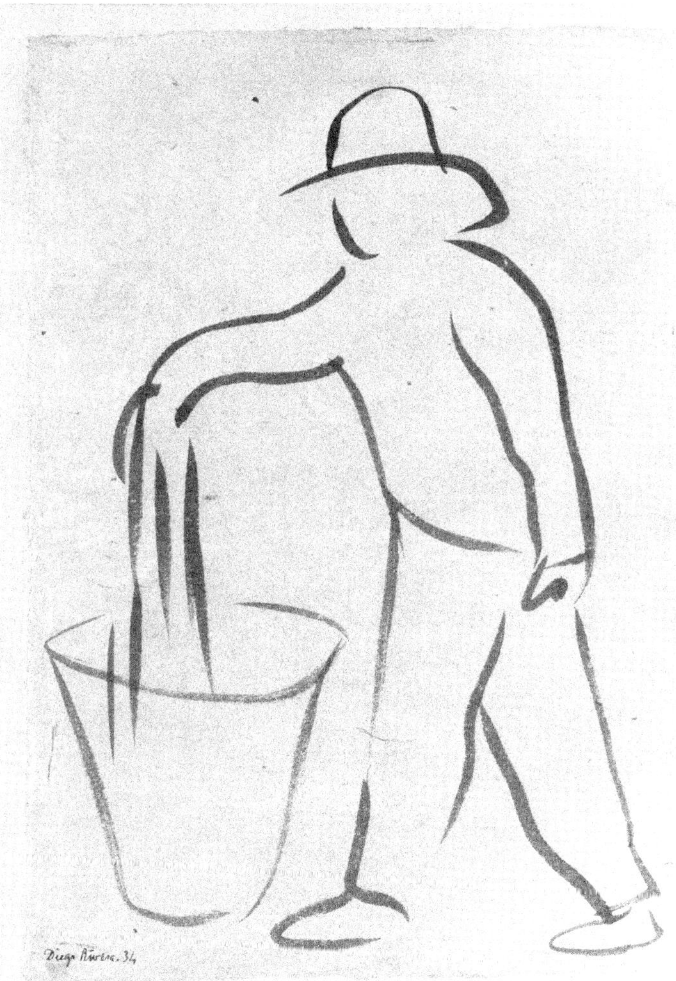

Diego Rivera, *Young Boy with a Bucket*, 1934

AFTERWORD

TRANSLATING ALFREDO'S interviews with Diego Rivera was a labor of love for Alvaro, the fulfillment of a promise he had made his brother in 1971 and did not get to until 2015–2016. He then spent many weeks painstakingly capturing both Alfredo's and Diego's words, moods, and intentions.

Half-brothers, they were ten years apart in age. Alfredo was no doubt a hero to the younger Alvaro. Although born in El Salvador, the brothers were raised for some years in Costa Rica by their paternal aunts. Alvaro had many stories of his brother's escapades from that time. Apparently, Alfredo was a handful—a bright and entertaining one, but difficult for his maiden aunts.

As adults, the brothers saw each other infrequently, but maintained a close and loving relationship, often exchanging letters and their various publications. Both were poets and writers with great respect for one another's work. In 1977, they collaborated on bilingual elegies for their father, each translating the other's poem, Alfredo with the help of a translator since he spoke little

English himself. It was published in 1977 under the title *Dos Elegias/Two Elegies*.

I met Alfredo in the early 1970s and again several more times when he visited California and once when we visited his home in Mexico City. Although neither of us spoke the other's language well enough to converse, I felt, from Alvaro's admiration and respect for his brother, as though I did indeed know him as the fine poet and writer he was, as well as the man-about-town with a freewheeling attitude toward life. Energetic and clearly highly observant, filled with enthusiasm for everything around him, Alfredo was a bit like a whirlwind whenever he came to visit. I can't imagine a more suitable interviewer for Diego Rivera.

—Barbara McCauley Cardona,
wife of the late Alvaro Cardona-Hine,
Truchas, New Mexico. Fall 2017

ABOUT THE AUTHOR

ALFREDO CARDONA PEÑA (1917–1995) was a poet, narrator, essayist, journalist, and science fiction writer from Costa Rica, considered one of the greatest Latin American authors of the 20th century. He lived in Mexico from 1939 until his death in 1995, and his literary, journalistic, and educational work was carried out mainly in Mexico City. He became a widely-read columnist with access to key figures of the artistic and intellectual scene of Mexico's capital. His fearsome Chronicles column in *El Nacional* earned him reputation as an analyst of the cultural times, and his weekly interviews with the controversial muralist Diego Rivera, from which this book derives, were an overwhelming success.

Cardona Peña also wrote for Costa Rican newspapers *La Nación* and the *Universidad Seminar*, and authored short stories in various genres from fairy tales to horror and science fiction. Humor and sharp irony were his specialty. He also taught at the National University of Mexico.

Cardona Peña's numerous awards include the Central American Award, twice the National Literary Prize of Costa Rica, the Magón Culture Prize in Costa Rica, and, in Mexico, the Alfonso Reyes Prize for short story and the National Prize of Campeche. He also earned awards in Guatemala and in the United States, where he was given the Continental Poetry Award by the American Atheneum of Washington.